HINTS ON NATIONAL EDUCATION IN INDIA

HINTS ON NATIONAL EDUCATION IN INDIA

BY

SISTER NIVEDITA OF RK. V.

GYAN

Published by

Gyan Publishing House
5, Ansari Road
Daryaganj, New Delhi-110002
Phone: 011-47034999, 9811692060
E-mail: books@gyanbooks.com

Distribution Network
gyanbooks.com
India, USA, Canada, UK, Australia

ISBN: 978-81-212-7027-4 (PB)
First Published, 1923

2nd Impression 2024

Printed at: Gyan Press, Delhi.

HINTS ON NATIONAL EDUCATION IN INDIA
Author: SISTER NIVEDITA OF RK. V.

HINTS ON NATIONAL EDUCATION IN INDIA

BY

SISTER NIVEDITA OF RK.-V.

CONTENTS.

FOREWORD.

The writings of the late Sister Nivedita in the awakening of a sense of want for national education among our countrymen and the implanting of civic interests in their hearts have already received recognition everywhere as being quite extraordinary and deeply suggestive in their nature. Indeed, it is, as the late Sir Rash Behari Ghosh, in a mood of Hebraic vision aptly remarked, on the day of the Memorial meeting held in the Town Hall, Calcutta, after her passing away, that "If the dead bones are beginning to stir to-day it is because the Sister Nivedita has breathed the breath of life into them." How much of truth is there imbedded in this assertion, it is for the posterity to judge, but we, who are so much distracted to-day and are casting about for a national life-principle, a saving evangel that is to rescue us out of the rut of stagnation we are experiencing on every side—and nowhere more helplessly than in the sphere of education—might do well to pay heed to this balm of inspiration which was the late Sister's special prerogative in life to administer to our drooping national consciousness and our fast-fleeting national vigour. She has, following in the footsteps of her great Master, advised us herein to be men among men, to hold our heads high, in thought, word and deed, so that the glory and grandeur that were *Bharata-varsha*, in a sense far surpassing the glory that was Greece, or the grandeur that was Rome, in their own heyday, might find their resplendent home among us once more and draw all the rest of the world to Her. Sad to say, however, she did not live to give us her complete thinking on the subject of education, which was so much near and dear to her heart, but only succeeded in giving us the faint, but by no means therefore, weak, outlines of how to adapt our life and our education through it to the Ideal—our national Ideal, from day to day, and thus ended in the overture what otherwise should have followed it, a grand and finished symphony of our national life-programme.

The present compilation of some of her writings on matters of education, now more appropriately styled "National Education in India", was first published as a booklet under the title: 'Hints on Education.' It has been thought fit here, now, to add to those, some of her other very illuminating and helpful contributions on this head, which she wrote for the *Modern Review* and the *Karma-Yogin*,—the last journal, a long since defunct one. The incorporation is due to the fact that these have materially a close bearing on the recent, widely discussed topic of national education, what it is and what its aims and ideals should be, and we gratefully acknowledge our indebtedness to these two journals, in respect of the use we have made of the Sister's articles in them. The paper on "Manual Education" was published long ago in pamphlet form, and so was the 'Project for the Ramkrishna Girls' School,' written so far back as 1900, when the Sister was in America trying to raise a fund for the starting of her school here, which she eventually succeeded in doing on a small scale. The importance of including these and two of the other papers besides,—that on Historical Research and on Co-operation, being of a somewhat personal nature at first, written to two very eminent scholars—along with the rest, almost as they were first published, is here justified if only because they are still to be found to be very broad in their application and very far-reaching in the efforts sought to be brought about, though the details recorded in at least two of them may seem to vary to some extent now. It is very needless indeed for us to point out how much of her inner conviction the Sister always tried to bring forth and succeeded in so doing, in her writings on such subjects as those herein included. But the least we can say about them, the least we are sure of them is this that the message and the directions which she has imparted to us so splendidly in these pages should certainly be held in their total effect in the same light as Ralph Waldo Emerson's measuring of the American scholar is and has been in the Western hemisphere, as the charter of India's intellectual freedom, even as the other is that of the United States of America.

HINTS ON
NATIONAL EDUCATION IN INDIA

PRIMARY EDUCATION: A CALL FOR PIONEERS.

We all know that the future of India depends, for us, on education. Not that industry and commerce are unimportant, but because all things are possible to the educated, and nothing whatever to the uneducated man. We know also that this education, to be of any avail, must extend through all degrees, from its lowest and humblest applications, up to the highest and most disinterested grades. We must have technical education and we must have also higher research, because technical education, without higher research, is a branch without a tree, a blossom without any root. We must have education of women, as well as education of men. We must have secular education, as well as religious. And, almost more important than any of these, we must have education of the people, and for this, we must depend upon ourselves.

Our civilisation has never been backward in bringing to the notice of the individual his responsibility to the society. There is none so poor that has never tried to feed the starving. From this time we must recognise the still greater urgency of giving knowledge. There is no other way of making the unity of our country effective. If one class of the people derive all their mental sustenance from one set of ideas, and the bulk of the population from something else, this unity, although certainly present, cannot easily be made effective. But if all the people talk the same language, learn to express themselves in the same way, to feed their realisation upon the same ideas, if all are trained and equipped to respond in the same way to the same forces, then our unity will stand self-demonstrated, unflinching. We shall have acquired national solidarity, and power of prompt and intelligent action. In this very fact, of universal education, the goal will have been attained, and none could succeed in turning us back.

Nor need we regret that we fall back, for this, upon our own strength. Education for the people is, in the first place, reading, writing and arithmetic. As long as we carry the burden ourselves, there need be no juggling with the geographical distribution of languages. But for artificial intervention, Orissa, Bengal and Behar might now have been talking a single tongue, using a single script, quoting from a great consolidated literature. We must do all we can for the simplification of the language-problem, and for this, nothing could be so effective as our own feeble action, infinitely preferable to the centralised, mechanical organisation.

Another advantage in our own effort is, that it alone can be a permanent force. It depends upon no outside influence. Let the centralisers come and go, and change as they will, the initiative that resides in the nerve-ends themselves, remains in tact, can never be infringed.

We have to build up this idea of the sacred duty of giving education to the people as one of the elements of our civilisation. Already we have the idea of giving alms. The one is only an extension of the other.

In most western countries, it is required that every young man, when his education is complete, shall give three, four, or five years to military service. He goes into barracks, is regimented, and drilled, makes a unit in the standing army, and passes out, usually, when his term is ended, an efficient soldier, to remain, for the rest of his life, ready at any moment to join in the armed defence of his country.

What we have to do, is in like fashion, to organise the army of education. Why should it be thought impossible that every student, when his own education is over, should be called upon to give three years to the people? It is of course understood that just as the only son of a widow is in the west excused military service, so one whose earnings are absolutely necessary to others must be excused the educational service. The villagers, on the other hand, would easily maintain a single student, living amongst them as a school-master. And when his own three years were over, it is to be supposed that he could, from his own old school or college, arrange for another to take his place. Some would learn to love the simple village life, and elect to live and die, poor school-masters. Most, however, would serve the years of their vow, and pass on, returning to the city, to bear their part in the life of a more complex community. On the one hand, the duty of teaching, on the other, the duty of maintaining, so teacher and taught make the perfect social unit. And so the great masses of the people might be swept within the circle of articulation. It takes thirty years to make a whole people literate, even supposing that an idea like this were carried out in its fullness. But with it we must not neglect the Asiatic device that makes every morsel of social service self-supporting and self-propagating. India never forgets to wing the seed that she has brought to ripeness. Along with the teaching must go the awaking of responsibility for further teaching. "Alms to the teacher," and "Knowledge to the people," must be converse truths, taught at one and the same time.

No state central organisation could arrange a scheme like this. Only by a common impulse of the people and the students themselves could it be made a reality. But it is not impossible. The initial thought comes, it is true, from the city, but once sent out, all depends upon the number of lives that can be laid upon its altar. All must always in the last resort depend upon this, the quantity and quality of human life that can be sacrificed to it. Without men's lives, no seed of the mind germinates. How many will give up comfort, place, opportunity, ease, even perhaps their whole life, for this, the elementary education of the Indian people?

PAPER ON EDUCATION—I.

The education that we give our children inevitably expresses our own conception of that synthesis of which our lives form a part. Thus, the American school will consider itself incomplete, until it has found out how to initiate the youth into mechanical processes. The Australian school will probably strive to lay the foundations of agriculture. The schools of a scientific age will recognise the importance of science, and those of a classical revival, that of dead languages. It follows that two different ages will never repeat each other exactly, in the matter of education, for the simple reason that in different historical epochs, nations select different branches of training, as of central necessity to their children, really because they are paramount factors for the moment, in the national life.

In Bengal, for instance, under the Sanskrit Renascence of the Guptas, a knowledge of the Sanskrit language and literature became the distinctive mark of a gentleman. A thousand years later, a man in the same position had to be versed in Persian also. To-day, English is the test. Thus a similar mental and social dignity is atained by changing means, at different epochs.

Fortunately for the civilisation of India, the Hindu has always clearly perceived the mind behind the method, as the thing with which education has fundamentally to deal. It is this which, in spite of so many catastrophes, has, in the past, saved the Indian genius from destruction. And it is this which constitutes its best security for the future. Just so long as the Brahminic system of directly training the minds of the young to concentration persists, will the Indian people remain potentially equal to the conquest of any difficulty that the changing ages may bring them. But once let this training be neglected or lost, and in spite of purity of race, the vigour of the Indian mind would probably fall to a level with that of modern peoples in general, waxing and waning with the degree and freedom of self-expression that the passing period might permit them. At present—owing largely to the peculiar psychological discipline, received by girls as well as boys, along with their devotional training—the most salient characteristic of the Hindu intellect is its reserve of strength, its conservation of power. As we read the history of the country, we are amazed at the unforeseenness with which geniuses occur, and the brilliance of their isolated achievements. The Indian Bhaskaracharya in the twelfth century, envisages the fact of gravitation with as unflinching a conviction—though social conditions do not lead him to so clear an enunciation—as the Western Newton, in the seventeenth. A race of women, cloistered and secluded, blossom forth suddenly into a Chand Bibi. Within the last twenty years, in spite of universal clerkship, we have given to the world men who have enriched humanity in Religion, in Science, and in Art. The invention of smokeless powder, and improvements made in surgery, are extended *applications* of knowledge, merely. India has shown herself potent to add to knowledge itself.

These things are some indication of the sleeping power of the Indian mind. They are the chance blossoms that show the living-ness of the whole tree. They tell us that what Indian people have done in the past, that Indian people can do in the future. And if it be so, then we owe this undying vitality to the fact that whatever may have been the characteristic expression most prized, at any given moment, our forefathers never neglected the culture and development of the mind itself. The training of the attention—rather than the learning of any special subject, or the development of any particular faculty—has always been, as the Swami Vivekananda claimed for it, the chosen goal of Hindu education. Great men have been only as incidents, in the tale of this national effort, to achieve control and self-direction of the mind itself.

It is not here, then, in the object and nature of the inner psychological process, that Western educators have anything to teach India. Instead of this, the superiority of the West lies in her realisation of the value of great united efforts in any given direction,—even that of self-education—and in the particular synthesis which, as she may think, it is necessary for the educational process to reflect. Thus, India may, all things considered, be capable of producing a greater number of geniuses, per thousand of her population, than Germany or America : but Germany and America have known how to bring *the national mind* to bear on their respective problems! That is to say, they have organised the common, popular mind, and to this organised mind they have presented the riddle that is to be guessed. Let us think of the mental weight and area, the material quantity and power, so to speak, of the thought thus brought in contact with the question they want answered. What is that question? Very probably it is strictly relative in its character. We may perhaps assume, without injustice, that it is the prosperity and well-being of their respective country and people, only. This is no impersonal, no absolute goal, such as that Renunciation and *Mukti* which India proposes to her children. Quite true. And yet, to the mind and soul of the individual German or American the prosperity of his country will appear as an impersonal end. Even the Hindu has to begin climbing towards renunciation in the abstract, by first practising self-suppression, for the sake of others, in the concrete. Even to the Hindu, the thought of the family is apt to be the first, as it were, of "those altar-stairs that slope through darkness up to God." Those dependent on him, he will say if we ask him, are a trust put into his hands, as a means whereby to work out his own *karma*, and reach true discrimination. And why should the German and the American not feel the same thing about their own countries? Why should this not be to them the last great step in "the altar-stairs" of life?

Supposing that it is so, the individual of each nation must be able to pursue the studies necessary to the earning of a livelihood, with the idea before him of a noble devotion to the cause of his people as a whole. Not cherishing this idea, he would still have had to prepare himself for a life of earning—even the Hindu has to do that! with the difference that he could not then have put into his training or his service all the ardour of motive, or all the lofty imagination of which he is capable. There is nothing so belittling to the human soul, as the acquisition of knowledge, for the sake of worldly reward. There is nothing so degrading to a nation, as coming to look upon the life of the mind as a means to bread-winning. Unless we strive for truth because we love it, and must at any cost attain, unless we live the life of thought out of our own rejoicing in it, the great things of heart and intellect will close their doors to us. There is a very definite limit to the distance a man can go, under the impulsion of a worldly motive. But if, on the other hand, his very love for those dear to him, is on a plane so lofty and so true that it presents itself to him as a reason for being and reaching the utmost possible ; if he knows that the more he can realise, the better will it be, if not for his own immediate family, yet for that wider kindred that he calls his country, then his public spirit is of a quality to give him wings. It adds freedom, not bondage. It becomes an achievement, not a limitation.

In this matter, India may have something to learn from the West. Why should we limit the social motive to a man's own family, or to his own community? Why not alter the focus, till we all stand, aiming each at the good of all-the-others, and willing, if need be, to sacrifice himself, his family, and even his particular social group, for the good of the whole? The will of the hero is ever an impulse to self-sacrifice. It is for the good of the People—not for my own good that I should strive to become one with the highest, the noblest, and the most truth-loving that I can conceive. It may even work out to my own personal destruction. It may lead to my swimming across the flood, to carry on the work of the telegraph-station, or leaping into the pit of death, for the rescue of a comrade. Either might be fatal. Shall I leave my family to struggle with poverty, unprovided? Away with the little vision! Shall we not eagerly die, both I and they, to show to the world what the Indian idea of duty may be? May not a single household be glad to starve, in order that a nation's face may shine? The hero's choice is made in a flash. To him, the larger vision is closer than the near. Within an instant, he strikes for eternity, strikes and is done. In concentrating the individual mind on the national problem, the West makes a hero out of many a common man. This also is a form of realisation.

We have to think, then, of the concentration of the Indian mind on the Indian problem. In order to do this, we are not asked to abandon that older system of training the mind itself, and rendering it familiar with absolute and universal considerations, on which, as already said, so much that is distinctive in Indian power and culture has depended in the past, and must depend in the future. But whereas, at present, the great bulk of our popular mind is pre-occupied with schemes of instruction, for the purpose of earning individual livelihoods, we now desire to consider the best means for bringing about a conscious unification of that mind, in order that we may be better able to compass thereby the common weal, the good of the whole. This substitution of the common good for the particular good—with the result that a higher level of individual good is rendered possible—is a process whose practicability is evidenced in Europe herself. It is not on special personalities and rarely-equipped faculties that the course of European history depends to-day, so much as the weight and power of common mind that has been unified and released, to work on certain given tasks. It is so released, and prepared for such release, by the form and quality of popular education. It is for us, then, who are Indian, to see what are the essentials of that education, with a view to appropriating its benefits to India and the Indian people.

PAPER ON EDUCATION—II.

In a perfect education, we can easily distinguish three different elements not always chronologically distinct. First, if we would obtain from a human mind the highest possible return, we must recognise in its education the stage of preparing it to learn, of training it to receive impressions, of developing it intensively, as it were, independently of the particular branch of knowledge through which this is done. Of the very existence of this phase of the educational process, many are unaware.

Secondly, in all historic epochs, but preeminently in this modern age, there is a certain characteristic fund of ideas and concepts which is common to society as a whole, and must be imparted to every individual, who is to pass, in his mature life, as efficient. This is the element that is supposed in the common acceptance to be the whole of education. It bulks the largest. It costs the most labour. It is the process that it is most obviously impossible to eliminate. And yet it is really only one of three elements. And strange to say, it is the very one which is least essential to the manifestation of what we call genius. Never was there a period in the world's history, when this aspect of education was so large or imperative as to-day. 'Geography, history, algebra and arithmetic, all that mkes up the worry and fret of childish life, as some one said, are in reality the key to a glorious city. They are the franchise of the modern consciousness. Carrying them, a man has a basis of communication with the whole wide world of educated minds.

But thirdly, these two elements taken together, in their highest degree (and it is quite possible to be taken as 'educated', on a very modest allowance of the second, only!) will only prepare the mind for real education. They are nothing more than preliminary conditions. They are by no means the essential itself. Having them, the mind has become a fit instrument. But of what? What shall be its message? What is to constitute the burden of its education? What is it that so much preparation has prepared it for? The third element in a perfect human development sweeps away the other two. It takes note of them only by implication, as it were, in the higher or lower fitness of the mind itself. The man meets his *guru*, and devotes himself to a perfect passivity. Or he surrenders to some absorbing idea, which becomes the passion of his life. Or he takes up a pursuit, and lives henceforth for it, and it alone. The phase of the one has succeeded to the phase of the many. Regarded as a mind, the man has become a full human organism. He now stands a chance of contributing to the riches of humanity as a whole.

It is characteristic of India that it is the third and highest of these three elements that she has observed and analysed, allowing the other two to occur by accident. It is equally characteristic of the West that it is numbers one and two that she has observed and analysed, allowing number three to occur by accident!

Yet all three have their science, and certainly the last is not without it. Egoistic response to stimulus, constant mental activity, much restlessness and intellectual change of appetite, loud self-assertion, argumentativeness, and desire to manifest power, are apt to be the characteristics of a healthy second stage. But when the *guru* comes, or the idea that is to dominate the life is apprehended, there may be a keen initial struggle, but after it there is a period of profound apparent quiet. To see the thing as it appears to the mind of the master, is the one necessity. To serve him, acting as his hands and feet, as it were, in order that one's mind and heart may be made one with his ; to serve him silently, broodingly, with the constant attempt to assimilate his thought, this is the method. Throughout this period, there is no room for rebellion. Eventually the guru emancipates : he does not bind. It would be a poor service to him, if we felt compelled in his name to arrest the growth of an idea. Eventually we have to realise that the service to which he has called us is not his own, but that of Truth itself, and that this may take any form. But in the first place it is essential that we begin where he left off. In the first place, emptied of self, we have to labour to give expression to that idea which has struck root in us through him. We must understand that the whole significance of our own lives depends, first and last, on their relation to his life.

The *guru* may have remained hidden, and the disciple may stand in the blaze of the world. But every word, every gesture, will point the way to that secret sanctuary, whence comes his strength. For the greatest energy is imparted by the sense of working for the glory of another. No man could be so nobly ambitious for himself as his wife could be, for him. The very fact that it was for himself would undermine his sense of loftiness and inspiration. No disciple can win the same joy from spiritual independence, as from the enthusiasm of *guru-bhakti*. No son can feel so eager to make his own name famous, as he will be to magnify that of his father. These are amongst the deepest secrets of the human heart, and they form the area that India has chosen to explore. It is in this way that greatness is made.

It is difficult, however, in modern times,—and speaking in a sense more or less worldly,—difficult to recognise greatness, unless it speaks in the language of the second educational element. There is a certain fund of information which is more or less essential to the development and manifestation of modern personality. It is interesting to enquire, what are the essentials of this fund of information? But before we can enter into this, it may be advisable to consider the matter more as a whole. We can see that unselfishness is the real distinction *of fine persons*, of what Ramakrishna Paramhamsa might have called *Vidyâvân-lok*. In this sense, a peasant-woman may be greater than a reigning queen. Even in intellect, the farmer's wife may be the greater, for she may have keenness of judgment, discrimination, mother-wit, and a hundred powers in which the woman of rank and power is by no means her superior. Are the tales of the world's worship not of shepherds and dairy women, of carpenters and camel-drivers? But we can see that a mind whose field of activity is limited to some remote or obscure pursuit, has not the same chance of making its power felt, as one that is able to deal with those counters that the world as a whole recognises. Some Bhutia lad may be potentially a great poet, but he is likely to live and die mute and inglorious. The Homers and Shaksperes of history are partakers in the world-culture of their time.

And intellectual formulæ may be made a great help to moral development. We know that we ought to restrain our individual anger and impatience. But it is undoubtedly easier to do so, when we know something about the size and distance of the fixed stars, and can take refuge in the thought of the vastness of the cosmos. The growth of character can be much aided by intellectual activity, besides, requiring it in its maturity as a means of self-expression. We do not want to identify the mere drill of learning to read and write, and the memorising of a few facts conveyed by that vehicle, with the idea of culture. We are well aware that even literary culture might easily be greater in some illiterate Indian villager, familiar with *kathaks* and *mangol-gâyens* than in the most accomplished passer of examinations. But we do not wish, on the other hand, to forget that it is a duty to develop our intellectual powers. No Hindu, who wishes to fulfil his obligations to the *jana-desh-dharma* (जन-देश-धर्म), can afford to neglect any opportunity of learning that he can possibly make for himself. This is the daily sacrifice to the *Rishis,* and it is as binding on women as on men.

By emphasising the third educational element, are made the poets and scholars of the world. The idea before which we are passive, that we may absorb it, the idea that fills our lives henceforth, the idea to which all our education has only been preparatory, this is the idea that is spirituality itself. Our self-subordination here is renunciation. Our enthusiasm here is an apostolate. It matters nothing about the form of expression. Our whole character is bathed in the river of this intellectual passion to emerge new, radiant, self-restrained, and self-directed. The only sin is to expect a return to ourselves, in riches, or honour, or fame. But the man who has really entered into the great life of ideas is not long held back, or seriously embittered by this childishness, for the energy of his pursuit dominates him, and excludes even himself from his thought. Palissy the potter was such an idealist. So was Stephenson, who invented the railway engine. Newton, boiling his watch instead of an egg, was a third. A nation stands or falls, in the long run, by the number of such souls that she is capable of producing, out of the rank and file of ordinary education. What about India, in this respect, to-day? Let the army of her poor scholars answer! Let the capacity of her people for universal ideas answer! Let the trumpet-call of Advaita, on the lips of Vivekananda answer! Science, art, history, the crafts, business, the development of men on planes external and internal, all these are but so many different expressions of That One. Through any of them may come the flood of light, the shaping and moulding of character, the infinite self-forgetting that means the goal itself. To have a chance of this, the idea must be stated. The ideal must be consciously held. Common education must be reverenced as a sacrament, making the opportunity for this exaltation and consecration. And if we once grasp these things, we shall see that we have no choice, that the education of all, the People as well as the classes, woman as well as man,—is not to be a desire with us, but lies upon us as a command. Humanity is mind, not body—

soul, not flesh. Its heritage is in the life of thought and feeling. To close against any the gates of the higher life is a sin far greater than that of murder, for it means responsibility for spiritual death, for inner bondage, and the result is ruin unspeakable. There is but one imperative duty before us to-day. It is to help on Education by our very lives if need be—Education in the great sense as well as the little, in the little as well as in the big.

PAPER ON EDUCATION—III.

Our conception of education must have a soul. It must form a unity. It must take note of the child as a whole, as heart as well as mind, will as well as mind and heart. Unless we train the *feelings* and the *choice*, our man is not educated. He is only decked out in certain intellectual tricks that he has learnt to perform. By these tricks he can earn his bread. He cannot appeal to the heart, or give life. He is not a man at all ; he is a clever ape. Learning, in order to appear clever, or learning, in order to earn a livelihood,—not in order to become a man, to develop one's own manhood and manliness,—means running into this danger. Therefore, in every piece of information that is imparted to a child, we must convey an appeal to the heart. At every step in the ascent of knowledge, the child's own will must act. We must never *carry* the little one upwards and onwards ; he must himself struggle to climb. Our care must be to put just so much difficulty in his way as would stimulate his will, just so little as to avoid discouragement. When, within and behind the knowledge gained, there stands *a man,* there stands *a mind*, then the task of instruction can be changed into one of self-education. The taught is now safe, he will teach himself. Every boy sent abroad is sent, on the understanding that he is in this sense developed. He is thrown into the moral ocean to battle for himself with the waves of difficulty and of temptation. We *assume* that he is a swimmer. But what have we done to ensure it?

There is one way, and one way only. It is, throughout the early years of education, to remember that there is nothing so important as the training of the *feelings*. To feel nobly, and to choose loftily and honestly, is a thousandfold more important to the development of faculty than any other single aspect of the educational process. The lad in whom this power is really present and really dominant, will always do the best thing possible under any given circumstances. The boy in whom it is not present is liable to confusion of the will, and confusion may mean only error, or it may mean demoralisation.

Very few parents and teachers amongst us at present have thought much of the pre-eminent necessity and importance of this training of the heart. What is it then that we trust to, for our children, in a fashion so blind? We trust, more or less unconsciously, to the general action of home, family, religion, and country, on the conscience and the emotions. It is the immense moral genius of the Indian people as a whole that has really formed so many fine men out of the students of the past two or three generations. And it is the crucial importance of the element in the environment that makes the foreign educator so undesirable. Our own countryman, however unversed in educational theory, is likely to be in harmony with our highest emotional life. His chance words will touch the keys of spiritual motive, where the best-intentioned foreigner with all his efforts, is liable to fail. The man who could not deliberately awaken the great formative influences, may do so by accident, if he and we are sufficiently of one world. The chance is very small that a stranger will even dream of the need for doing so. It is almost true that the worst of ourselves is a better schoolmaster for us, than the best of another people.

Having once recognised the law, however, we are no longer at the mercy of circumstances. The home can see to it that the school builds up the child. Even an ignorant mother, by teaching her boy to love, and to act on his love, can be the finest of educators. It is this that makes so many of our great men of to-day, attribute so much to their mothers. The old education of the girl, by the *brata*, is full of this appeal to the heart, as the only sound basis of education. But modern education, in its first inception, ignored this factor altogether, and thus produced faculty out of relation to its environment. Henceforth, the Indian people will not repeat this error. Henceforth they will understand—indeed they have understood for several years past—that even schooling has to justify itself to the conscience of the schooled, by the great law of sacrifice, and that this law here is, the development of the child for the good, not of himself, but of *jana-desha-dharma* (जन-देश-धर्म) or, as the western would phrase it, the development of the individual for the benefit of the environment. 'Why are you going to school?' says the mother to her little one, at the moment of parting. And the child answers, in some form or other, growing clearer and more eager with growing age and knowledge. 'That I may learn to be a man, AND HELP!' There is no fear of weakness and selfishness for one whose whole training has been formed round this nucleus.

This, the desire to serve, the longing to better conditions, to advance our fellows, to lift the whole, is the real religion of the present day. Everything else is doctrine, opinion, theory.

Here is the fire of faith and action. Each day should begin with some conscious act of reference to it. A moment of silence, a hymn, a prayer, a salutation, any of these is ritual sufficient. It is not to the thing worshipped, but to ourselves, that our worship is important! Any symbol will do, or none. It is for this that our fathers have bidden us worship the water of the seven sacred rivers, or the earth of holy places, the footsteps of the *guru*, or the name of the Mother. All these are but suggestions to the mind, of the *jana-desha-dharma* (जन-देश-धर्म) to which we dedicate ourselves, whose service is the motive-spring of all our struggles. "No man liveth to himself alone." In proportion as we realise this, can be the greatness of our living. In proportion as it is our motive, will be the reality of our education.

PAPER ON EDUCATION—IV.

Education in India to-day, has to be not only national, but NATION-MAKING. We have seen what a national education is—a training which has a strong colour of its own, and begins by relating the child to his home and country, through all that is familiar, but ends by making him *free of all* that is true, cosmopolitan, and universal. This is the necessary condition of all healthy education, in all countries, whatever their political position or stage of development. These general statements are as true of England and France, as of India, as true in happiness as in adversity.

The need for special attention to nation-making, however, is a question of the moment, a matter of those temporary vicissitudes through which a country may be passing, in a given period. It is always easy, by common consent of responsible persons, or by the sound communal instincts of a healthy people, to select out and emphasise, for a definite purpose, any elements in a general education that may be thought desirable. All our institutions have arisen in some such way. The need of purity was first brought forward, in our customs, at some time when loss of civilisation was a pressing danger. The regulation of marriage was a device deliberately intended to prevent mixture of race, in a period that had to face this as a possibility. Similarly, a people who need above all things the development of a national sense, can make special provision for developing the necessary elements of thought and character, throughout the education of their children.

National feeling is, above all, feeling for others. It is rooted in public spirit, in a strong civic sense. But these are only grandiloquent names for what may be described as organised unselfishness. The best preparation for nation-making that a child can receive is to see his elders always eager to consider the general good, rather than their own. A family that willingly sacrifices its own interests to those of the village, or the street, or the town ; a household that condones no act of dishonesty on the part of public servants, out of consideration for its own comfort or safety ; a father who will fling himself at any obstacle, in the cause of honour and justice for the people, these are the best and strongest education for nation-making that a child can have. The wild-boar, small as he is, throws himself upon the horse and his rider, never doubting his own capacity to destroy both.

This is the courage of the man who attacks public evils. This is the object-lesson by which a child can best be trained. Hunger for the good of others, as an end in itself, the infinite pity that wakes in the heart of an Avatar, at sight of the suffering of humanity, these are the seed and root of nation-making. We are a nation, when every man is an organ of the whole, when every part of the whole is precious to us ; when the family weighs nothing, in comparison with the People.

China in Asia, and France in Europe, are the two countries that have best known how to make the public spirit into religion. This is the fact that made Joan of Arc a possibility. A peasant-girl in a remote village could brood over the sorrows of her country, till she was possessed by the feeling that "there was much pity in Heaven for the fair realm of France". An idea like this was like the compassion of a Buddha, and nowhere but in France could it have been applied to the country.

We must surround our children with the thought of their nation and their country. The centre of gravity must lie, for them, outside the family. We must demand from them sacrifices for India, *bhakti* for India, learning for India. The ideal for its own sake. India for the sake of India. This must be as the breath of life to them. We must teach them about India, in school and at home. Some lessons must fill out the conception, others must build up the sense of contrast. Burning love, love without a limit. Love that seeks only the good of the beloved, and has no thought of self, this is the passion that we must demand of them.

We must teach them to think heroically. They must be brought up to believe in their own people. Few stories are so moving as that of two English youths who were killed by an angry mob in the Punjab, dying with the words on their lips, "We are not the last of the English!" Similarly we must learn to draw every breath in the proud conviction, "We are not the last of the Indians!" This faith our children must inherit from us, along with all other forms of stern and heroic thought. It is a mistake to think heroes are born. Nothing of the sort. They are made, not born; made by the pressure of heroic thought. All human beings long at bottom for self-sacrifice. No other thirst is so deep as this. We desire destruction, not prosperity, and the good of others.

Let us recognise this. Let us make room for it. Let us emphasise it, and direct it towards one single *bhakti*. Let love for country and countrymen, for People and Soil, be the mould into which our lives flow hot. If we reach this, every thought we think, every word of knowledge gained, will aid in making clearer and clearer the great picture. With faith in the Mother, and *bhakti* for India, the true interpretation of facts will come to us unsought. We shall see the country as united, where we were told that she was fragmentary. Thinking her united, she will actually be so. The universe is the creation of mind, not matter. And can any one force in the world resist a single thought, held with intensity by three hundred millions of people? Here we have the true course of a nation-making education.

PAPER ON EDUCATION—V.

The reconstitution of a nation has to begin with its ideals. This, because in a nation three primary elements have to be considered, first the country, or region, second, the people, and third, the national mind. Of the three, the last is dominant, and all-directing. By working through it, we may modify or even re-create either or both of the other two while their influence upon it is comparatively feeble and indirect. Mind can re-make any thing, however inert or rebellious, but a rebellious mind, what can reach? It follows that in national *reconstruction* there is no other factor so important as education. How is this to be made national and nationalising? What is a national education? And conversely, what is un-national? And further what kind of education offers the best preparation for the attempt to solve the national problems? What type of education would be not only national, but also nation-making?

Education has to deal with various factors, the imparting of special processes, the assimilating of certain kinds and quantities of knowledge, the development of the man himself. Of all these it is the last which is incomparably the most important, and in the man, it is again his ideals which form the critical element. It is useless to attempt to teach a man anything which he does not desire to learn. It is absurd to try to force on him an advantage which he resists. Education is like mining. It begins with the ideal, it builds first at the top.

New ideals have to be approached through the old. The unfamiliar has to be reached through the familiar. It may indeed be questioned whether there is such a thing as a *new* ideal. There is an ideal and there is a form through which it is expressed, but when we reach the ideal itself, we have reached the eternal. Here, all humanity is at one. Here, there is neither new nor old, neither own nor foreign. The limiting forms are some old, some new, but the ideal itself knows nothing of time. Yet the expression "new ideals" has a certain meaning. European poetry, for instance, glorifies and exalts the betrothed maiden. Indian poetry equally idealises the faithful wife. Both are only customary forms through which is reached the supreme conception, that of holiness in woman. Obviously, however, it would be futile to try to lead the imagination of an Indian child to this ideal, through the characteristically

European conception, and equally foolish to try to lead the European child through the prevailing Indian form. Yet, when education has done its perfect work, in the emancipation of the imagination towards great and gracious womanhood, it is clear that there will be an instant apprehension of this ideal, even in new forms. The poetry of Tennyson and Browning will at once be understood as its highest and best, by the trained and developed heart and yet it would have been a crime to try to bring up the Indian child on it. Equal would be the folly of trying to educate the European child on Sita and Savitri instead of Beatrice and Joan of Arc, although the same child when grown up, may well test the depth of its own culture by its instant sympathy with the Eastern heroines.

A national education is, first and foremost, an education in the national idealism. We must remember, however, that the aim of education is emancipation of sympathy and intellect. This is not often reached by foreign methods. But in the exceptional cases of a few individuals it may seem to occur; and better emancipation through the foreign, than bondage through our own! By this fact of the attainment of the universal, must the education ultimately stand justified, or condemned. To emancipate the greatest number of people most easily and effectively, it is necessary to choose familiar ideals and forms, and in every case, it is necessary to make progression absolutely continuous, so that there be no sharp incongruity amongst the elements of early experience. Such incongruity begets confusion of thought, and this confusion is educational chaos. A national education then, must be made up of familiar elements. The ideals presented must always be first clothed in a form evolved by our own past. Our imagination must be first based on our own heroic literature. Our hope must be woven out of our history. From the known to the unknown, from the easy to the difficult, must be the motto of every teacher, the rule of every lesson. The familiar is not the goal ; knowledge is the goal : trained faculty is the aim. An education that stopped short at the familiar would be a bondage instead of an emancipation ; a mockery not a reality. The familiar is merely the first step. But as the first step, it is essential.

Geographical ideas must be built up first through the ideas of India. But they must not stop there. A knowledge of geography would be singularly rustic, if it did not include a clear concept of the world, as a whole. And even this is not sufficient. There must, in a complete education, be a release of the geographical faculty, an initiation into geographical enquiry, an inception of geographical research.

Similarly of history. The sense of historic sequence must be trained through India. To that, every thing else historical must stand related. But the history of India must be only a stepping-stone to constantly-widening circles of knowledge. The history of Mongolian, Semitic, European and African peoples ; their civilisations and their movements, must all be followed up. And the crown of this training will be found in the power to interpret anew the old facts, to perceive fresh significance, and unthought of sequences, and to gather from the story of the past the dynamic forces of the future.

So much for the historical education. It must never be forgotten that nationality in culture is the means, not the end. There is a level of achievement where all the educated persons of the world can meet, understand and enjoy each other's associations. This level is freedom. Intellectually speaking, it is *mukti*. But it can be reached only by him whose knowledge is firm-rooted in love for mother and mother-land, in tender memories of childhood and the early struggle, after knowledge, and in an unshakable assurance that the face of God shines brightest and His name sounds sweetest, in the village of his birth.

THE PLACE OF FOREIGN CULTURE IN A TRUE EDUCATION.

There is a great difference between a child's relation to his own family and to that of the great man of the village, in which he may be kindly received. Let us suppose the child's own father and mother and family, to be blotted out, and nothing substituted for them save the more formal terms of a guest in the richman's house. What a blank the emotional life of the child has become! His feelings have no natural root. The sense of the world has no centre within himself where he can rest, and feel that he has found the home of the soul. The external is not in organic continuity with an internal, in his life. Nothing can ever again equal, for any of us, the sense of being enfolded in the old old associations of our babyhood, in the arms where we lay, in the hour of our first awakening to the world, our childhood's home.

Every outer ought to be a direct branching out from some inner. The mind that is fed from the beginning on foreign knowledge and ideas, not rooted and built upon the sense of intimacy, is like the waif brought up in the stranger's home. The waif may behave well and reward his benefactor, but this is apt to be the fruit of an intellectual notion of duty, not because, loving him, he could not help it.

Can foreign learning then ever be so deeply grafted upon the stem of a man's own development that it forms a real and vital part of his intellectual personality? We might as well ask, Is there no place for the king or the zamindar in the mind of a child who has his own father and mother?

Again, there is the question of our relation to what is foreign, when our own culture is perfect. There is such a thing as the emancipation of the heart. For instance, we cannot imagine a cultivated person, of whatever nationality, not feeling the beauty of the Tâj. Nor can we imagine a cultivated Hindu—whether he knows English or not, failing to enjoy some beautiful old wood-carved Madonna of Europe. The appeal of the highest poetry is universal. One of the supreme blossoms of culture is taste.

We notice here that the man coming to admire the Tâj is not a learner but is already mature. The Indian standing before the Madonna is not going to imitate her. He is there only to enjoy. This distinction is vital. In a true education the place of foreign culture is never at the beginning. All true development must proceed from the known to the unknown, from the familiar to the unfamiliar, from the near to the far.

In all learning we should try to give knowledge, only in answer to enquiry. This is the ideal. If we could attain it perfectly, every child would grow up to be a genius. But how can there be curiosity about truth that is not within our world? If we could realise how complex a process is the growth of knowledge in a child, how the question that school must answer, awakens in him at some unforeseen moment, at play, on the road, at home, in the family, then we should also understand that every branch of thought in which the full activity of the mind is to be looked for, must be knit up with the daily life. The American child can learn truthfulness from George Washington : the Hindu had far better learn it from Yudhisthira. The Hindu man may be thrilled by Shakespeare's Brutus. But he can appreciate him only in proportion as his own childhood has been fed on heroic political ideals that he could understand in his own home, and in the Mahabharata. There is no such thing in education as a pure idea. Pure ideas are attained by *paramahamsas*. The ideas of the child are inextricably entangled with the things he sees about him, with social institutions, and with his own acts. Hence a foreign medium of education must first be translated by him into the weird and wonderful forms, characteristic of his ignorance, and only after this, if it be so lucky, has it the chance to emerge as knowledge at all.

The difference here between knowledge and the results of knowledge, is vital. Knowledge is one. In pure knowledge, and therefore in science, there can be neither native nor foreign. Emotion on the other hand, is entirely a matter of locality. All form is purely local. Every man's heart has its own country. Therefore art, which is form infused with emotion, must always be strongly characteristic of the place, the people and the mental tradition, whence it has sprung. While the beautiful is one, and art the unveiler of the beautiful, that art must nevertheless always be distinguishable as of this area or that. Knowledge is a duty, art is an enjoyment. For this reason we should give infinite searching of heart to the question of the place that foreign art may hold in a true education. And by art let it here be understood that we refer, above all, to poetry, with its exotic forms of feeling ; drama ; sculpture that is guided by canons that are not ours ; music that we do not understand ;

and architecture that is modern, and apt to be cheap and gaudy. This not deeply and intimately *understanding* is of the essence of the whole question. We are insincere when we strive for a thing, not because we already love it, but because we believe that it ought to be admired. And this kind of insincerity may creep into any action or opinion, even into so simple a thing as the choosing of a jewel, to make one's own character and personality seem vulgar and shoddy. 'Imitation', says Ruskin, 'is like prayer ; done for love it is beautiful, for show, horrible.

But have we no right to seek to extend our modes of feeling and forms of expression? This question may be answered by a reference to architecture. Fergusson points out in his great work that when the architecture of a people is great and living, they are all the better for accepting and assimilating minor elements of foreign origin. It matters very little, he tells us, whether the jewelled mosaics of the Indo-Saracenic style were or were not Italian in their origin, since India made of them something so singular in its beauty and so peculiarly her own. It is clear however that she could not have done this from the standpoint of an architecture that was itself a vague experiment. Because she knew thoroughly well what she liked, in her own building, therefore she knew what would be a beautiful ornament upon it. The dazed builder of to-day, working in forms with which he is unfamiliar, is by no means so fortunate, when he adorns them with crazy pottery or with monstrosities in the shape of artificial rockeries and many-coloured foliage!

Certainly we have a right to increase the area of our emotional experience. But, if we are sincere in this, it will be done only a little at a time, and as a result of toil and pain. Not by chattering about love, even though we do it in rhyme, can we become lovers! It is the delicacies, the renunciations, and the austerities of the great sentiments through which we extend the area of our experience, and not the gross caricatures of an easy pleasure-seeking. And there is none of us who seeks to have the sword in his own heart.

In all directions we find that only when deeply rooted in the familiar, may we safely take up the unfamiliar. In proportion as we rightly analyse the known, rightly distinguishing, even in what is familiar, between the ideal expressed and the form assumed, in that proportion will it open for us the book of the whole world. But in any case the man who does not love his own, the man who is not clear as to what is his own, will never be received by any people as anything more than half a man.

How much this comes home to one when one sees the futile efforts made by Indian parents to send their boys out into foreign countries to master the details of scientific industry! The seedling that has no root is transplanted to the wilderness for its growth! How clear it is that the one thing of all others that was necessary was a rooting and grounding in its own environment! In other words, before the lad left India, he ought first to have acquired the methods of science. Then, in the light of these methods he should have learnt all that India could have taught him, of the particular industry he was going out to master, in its simple and primitive *Swadeshi* form. Having weighed the primitive industry against his own modern schooling, having become aware of the gap between the two, having read all that he can find; having even experimented in so far as is possible, then let the lad be sent out, when his own mind is quivering with enquiry. Only when curiosity is already awakened, have we the energy to proceed from the known to the unknown.

I heard of a student who went to a foreign

country in the hope of learning from some farm how to make the printers' ink. Naturally enough, factory after factory refused him, and he had to return to India, having wasted his own efforts and his father's money, without the knowledge he went out to seek. This instance was particularly flagrant, because by India and China long ago was invented the very idea of durable inks, and because the knowledge of these is still so far from lost, that any manufacture of *Swadeshi* ink begun in a back lane to-day, can drive out of competition at once an equal quantity of the foreign writing-fluid of commerce. It follows that an Indian lad seeking to invent some form of printers' ink, with a moderate amount of intelligence and technological information, has a far better start than, fifty or sixty years ago, had the people from whom he now proposes to beg or steal. The whole trouble and loss arose in this case from a misconception of the place of foreign knowledge in a true scheme of education. It has no right to be, save as capstone and finial to a genuine, honest faculty and experience of indigenous growth.

Of course while this is said, and the ideal laid down so glibly for the individual, one remembers, with a pang, the ordeal that India as a whole has had to face. One remembers the unprecedented influx of foreign knowledge and foreign criticism, from the early decades of the nineteenth century onwards—an influx that has lost her many a mind and many a character that should have been amongst the noblest of her sons—an influx that only an extraordinary national integrity and self-determination could have enabled her to survive so long. While we remember this with fulness of comprehension and compassion, however, it is only the more binding upon us to walk warily in the matter of individual development ; for only by the bone and muscle of the individual, can we do aught to set right the wrong that has been done the whole.

Even in science, apart altogether from industry, it will only be those men who believe themselves to be inheriting and working out the greatest ideals of the Indian past, who will be able to lay one stone in the edifice of the national future,—if there is to be such an edifice at all. Not by the man who is working for his living, and wants it increased, that he may keep his wife and child in respectability and comfort ; not by the man who counts the cost ; not by the man who holds something back ; not by the man who strikes a bargain with ideals will the path of Indian science be 'blazed' through the forest. Asoka was the conqueror of Kalinga, and therefore the enemy of some of his people, till the bar sinister was wiped off his scutcheon by the message of Buddha, and he felt himself a man, and an Indian man, with a right to rule in greatness over his own empire. Even so will he who carries the torch of modern knowledge to the India of the future, be one who feels himself enfranchised of the whole greatness of Indian spirituality. That river of renunciation that courses through his will, must find its ocean indeed in Science. But Science will not stand suspect of that *bhakta* as less than the highest truth. Two things will contend in him,—the passion for truth, and the yearning over his own people in their ignorance. There will be no time for thought of *mukti* in that heart. Has the soldier thought of *mukti* when he follows his captain to the breach? A fire of sacrifice, without let or limit, will be the life that achieves this end. The form may be modern ; the name of science may be foreign ; but the life, the energy, the holiness of dedication will be Indian and know themselves for Indian. So to cease from the quest of *mukti* is *mukti* itself. Viewed in the light of such an impulse how mean and pitiful seems the effort at self-culture! The whole body of foreign knowledge can be assimilated easily by one thus rooted and grounded in his relation to his own country.

The anxiety for a theory of the right place of foreign culture too often clothes a mere desire for foreign *luxury*. With regard to this whole question, a man cannot have too severe a standard of self-respect. There was a time when men were born, either ravenous individuals, or at best, with the instincts of the pack. Today we cannot imagine a child in whom family honour is not a primitive instinct. It may be that ages will yet dawn in which the thought of motherland and countrymen will be as deeply inwrought in the human heart. To the men of that age how might the question look of the place of foreign luxuries in noble lives? Why should we not be 'anachronisms of the future,' using only what belongs to us or ours, by right of toil or moral conquest? Some standard of self-restraint and self-denial in these matters is demanded of every individual by his own need of moral dignity. The code that would use to the utmost not only all its opportunities but also all its chances, this code is too likely to turn Indian men into European women! Effeminacy is the curse that follows upon indulgence, even innocent indulgence, in foreign luxury. Frivolity, in moments of crisis, is the bane of the effeminate. One of the noblest of Christian adjurations lies in the words, "*Let us endure hardness*, as good soldiers of Christ;" and again the sublime exclamation, "Quit ye like men! Be strong." The inability to endure hardness, the inability to be earnest, the inability to play the man, either in action or devotion, in life or in imagination, these, if no worse, are the fruits of the tree of a luxury to which we have no right.

In the last and final court, it may be said, Humanity is one, and the distinction between native and foreign, purely artificial. The difference is relative. In a man's own country are many things foreign to his experience. With many a foreign luxury he has been familiar from his cradle. Morals, also it may be answered, are entirely relative. The difference between life and death, between victory and defeat, between excellence and degradation, are all entirely relative. By walking truly with discrimination through the world of the relative, do we grow to the understanding of such abstract and absolute ideas as the unity of Humanity. That unity makes itself known to the soul as a vast enfranchisement. It is never even dimly perceived by him who has taken the half for the whole, the outcast from human experience, the seeker after foreign ways and foreign thoughts, whose shame is his own mother,—*the man who has no native land.*

THE FUTURE EDUCATION OF THE INDIAN WOMAN

Here in India, the woman of the future haunts us. Her beauty rises on our vision perpetually. Her voice cries out on us. Until we have made ready a place for her, until we throw wide the portals of our life, and go out, and take her by the hand to bring her in, the Motherland Herself stands veiled and ineffective, with eyes lost, in set patience, on the earth. It is essential, for the joyous revealing of that great Mother, that she be first surrounded by the mighty circle of these, Her daughters, the Indian women of the days to come. It is they who must consecrate themselves before Her, touching Her feet with their proud heads, and vowing, to her their own, their husbands', and their children's lives. Then and then only will she stand crowned before the world. Her sanctuary to-day is full of shadows. But when the womanhood of India can perform the great *ârati* of nationality, that temple shall be all light, nay, the dawn verily shall be near at hand. From end to end of India, all who understand are agreed that the education of our women must needs, at this crisis, undergo some revision. Without their aid and co-operation none of the tasks of the present can be finally accomplished. The problems of the day are woman's as well as man's. And how idle were it to boast that our hearts are given to the Mother, unless we seek to enshrine Her in every one of our lives.

Indian hesitation, however, about a new type of feminine education, has always been due to a misgiving as to its actual aims, and in this the people have surely been wise. Have the Hindu women of the past been a source of shame to us, that we should hasten to discard their old-time grace and sweetness, their gentleness and piety, their tolerance and child-like depth of love and pity, in favour of the first crude product of Western information and social aggressiveness? On this point India speaks with no uncertain voice. "Granted," she says in effect, "that a more arduous range of mental equipment is now required by women, it is nevertheless better to fail in the acquisition of this, than to fail in the more essential demand, made by the old type of training, on character. An education of the brain that uprooted humility and took away tenderness, would be no true education at all. These virtues may find different forms of expression in mediæval and modern civilisations, but they are necessary in both. All education worth having must first devote itself to the developing and consolidating of character, and only secondarily concern itself with intellectual accomplishment."

The question that has to be solved for Indian women, therefore, is a form of education that might attain this end, of developing the faculties of soul and mind in harmony with one another. Once such a form shall be successfully thought out and its adequacy demonstrated, we shall, without further ado, have an era amongst us of Woman's Education. Each successful experiment will be the signal for a circle of new attempts. Already there is longing enough abroad to serve the cause of woman. All that we ask is to be shown the way.

Important to education as is the question of method, it is still only subordinate to that of purpose. It is our fundamental motive that tells in the development we attempt to give our children. It is therefore the more urgently necessary that in the training of girls we should have a clearly-understood ideal towards which to work. And in this particular respect, there is perhaps no other country in the world so fortunately placed as India. She is, above all others, the land of great women. Wherever we turn, whether to history or literature, we are met on every hand by those figures, whose strength she mothered and recognised, while she keeps their memory eternally sacred.

What is the type of woman we most admire? Is she strong, resourceful, inspired, fit for moments of crisis? Have we not Padmini of Cheetore, Chand Bibi, Jhansi Rani? Is she saintly, a poet, and a mystic? Is there not Meera Bae? Is she the queen, great in administration? Where is Rani Bhowani, where Ahalya Bae, where Janhabi of Mymensingh? Is it wifehood in which we deem that woman shines brightest? What of Sati, of Savitri, of the ever glorious Sita? Is it in maidenhood? There is Uma. And where in all the womanhood of the world, shall be found another as grand as Gandhari?

These ideals moreover are constructive. That is to say, it is not their fame and glory that the Indian child is trained to contemplate. It is their holiness, simplicity, sincerity, in a word, their character. This, indeed, is always a difference between one's own and an alien ideal. Impressed by the first, it is an effort that we seek to imitate: admiring the second, we endeavour to arrive at its results. There can never be any sound education of the Indian woman, which does not begin and end in exaltation of the national ideals of womanhood, as embodied in her own history and heroic literature.

But woman must undoubtedly be made *efficient*. Sita and Savitri were great in wifehood, only as the fruit of that antecedent fact, that they were great women. There was no place in life that they did not fill graciously and dutifully. Both satisfied every demand of the social ideal. At once queen and housewife, saint and citizen, submissive wife and solitary nun, as heroic combatant, both were equal to all the parts permitted them, in the drama of their time. Perfect wives as they were, if they had never been married at all, they must have been perfect just the same, as daughters, sisters, and disciples. This efficiency to all the circumstances of life, this womanhood before wifehood, and humanity before womanhood, is something at which the education of the girl must aim in every age.

But the moral ideal of the India of to-day has taken on new dimensions—the national and civic. Here also woman must be trained to play her part. And again, by struggling towards these she will be educated. Every age has its own intellectual synthesis, which must be apprehended, before the ideal of that age can be attained. The numberless pathways of definite mental concept, by which the orthodox Hindu woman must go to self-fulfilment, form, to the Western mind a veritable labyrinth. So far from being really un-educated, or non-educated, indeed, as is so commonly assumed, the conservative Hindu woman has received an education which in its own way is highly specialised, only it is not a type recognised as of value by modern peoples.

Similarly, in order to achieve the ideal of efficiency for the exigencies of the twentieth century, a characteristic synthesis has to be acquired. It is no longer merely the spiritual or emotional content of a statement that has to be conveyed to the learner, as in the mytho-logico-social culture of the past. The student must now seek to understand the limitations of the statement, its relation to cognate ideas and the steps by which the race has come to this particular formulation. The modern synthesis, in other words, is scientific, geographical, and historical, and these three modes of knowing must needs—since there is no sex in truth—be achieved by woman as by man.

Science, history and geography, are thus as

three dimensions in which the mind of the present age moves, and from which it seeks to envisage all ideas. Thus the conception of nationality—on which Indian efforts to-day converge—must be realised by us, in the first place, as a result of the study of the history of our own nation, with all its divergent elements of custom, race, language, and the rest. The civic sense, in the same way, must be reached by a study of our own cities, their positions, and the history of their changes from age to age.

Again, the nation must be seen, not only in relation to its own past, and its own place, but also, in relation to other nations. Here we come upon the necessity for geographical knowledge. Again, history must be viewed geographically and geography historically. A great part of the glory and dignity of the ideally modern woman lies in her knowledge that her house is but a tent pitched for a night on the star-lit world-plane, that each hour, as it passes, is but a drop from an infinite stream, flowing through her hand, to be used as she will, for benediction or for sorrow, and then to flow on irresistibly again. And behind such an attitude of mind, lies a severe intellectual discipline. But even the proportion which the personal moment bears to space and time, is not formula enough for the modern spirit. This demands, in addition, that we learn what is to it the meaning of the truth, or science, the fact in itself. This particular conception of truth is perhaps no more absolute than others, current in other ages, but it is characteristic of the times, and by those who have to pass the world's test, it has to be understood. Yet even this marked truth, thus thirsted after, has to be held as only a fragment of an infinitely extended idea, in which Evolution and Classification of the sciences play the parts of history and geography.

Nature, the Earth, and Time, are thus the three symbols by whose means the modern mind attains to possession of itself. No perfect means of using them educationally has ever been discovered or devised by man. The spirit of each individual is the scene of a struggle for their better realisation. Every school-room embodies an attempt to communalise the same endeavour. Those who would transmit the modern idea to the Indian woman, must begin where they can, and learn, from their own struggles, how better to achieve. In the end, the idea once caught, the Indian woman herself will educate Indian woman—meanwhile every means that offers ought to be taken. The wandering

Bhâgabatas or *Kathakas*, with the magic lantern, may popularise geography, by showing slides illustrative of the various pilgrimages. History outside the Mahabharata and Ramayana might be familiarised in the same way. And there is no reason why simple lectures on hygiene, sanitation, and the plants and animals of the environment should not also be given by the wandering teachers to the assembled community, with its women behind the screens. Pictures, pictures, pictures, these are the first of instruments in trying to concretise ideas, pictures and the mother-tongue. If we would impart a love of country, we must give a country to love. How shall women be enthusiastic about something they cannot imagine?

Schools large and small, schools in the home and out of it, schools elementary and advanced, all these are an essential part of any working out of the great problem. But these schools must be within Indian life, not antagonistic to it. The mind set between two opposing worlds of school and home, is inevitably destroyed. The highest ambition of the school must be to give moral support to the ideals taught in the home, and the home to those imparted in the school—the densest ignorance would be better for our women than any departure from this particular canon.

In making the school as much an essential of the girl's life, as it has always been of the boy's, we are establishing something which is never to be undone. Every generation as it comes will have to carry out the great task of the next generation's schooling. This is one of the constant and normal functions of human society. But much in the problem of Woman's Education as we to-day see it, is difficulty of the time only. We have to carry our country through an arduous transition. Once the main content of the modern consciousness finds its way into the Indian vernaculars, the problem will have disappeared, for we learn more from our Mother-tongue itself, than from all our schools and schoolmasters. In order to bring about that great day, however, the Mother Herself calls for vows and service of a vast spiritual knighthood. Hundreds of youngmen are necessary, to league themselves together for the deepening of education in the best ways amongst women. Most students, perhaps, might be able to vow twelve lessons in a year to be given either in home or village, during the holidays—this should hardly prove an exhausting undertaking—yet how much might be done by it.

Others might be willing to give themselves to the task of building up the vernacular literatures. The book and the magazine penetrate into recesses where the teacher's foot never yet trod. The library, or the book-self, is a mute university. How are women to understand Indian history, if, in order to read about Buddha or Asoka, about Chandragupta or Akbar, they have first to learn a foreign language? Great will be the glory of those hereafter who hide their ambition for the present, in the task of conveying modern knowledge in the tongues of women and the People?

Seeing that this first generation of pioneer-work must needs be done mainly by men, on behalf of women, there are some who would scoff at the possibility of such generosity and devotion. But those who know the Indian people deeply cannot consent to this sneer. Life in India is socially sound. Civilisation is organic, spiritual, altruistic. When the practice of *suttee* was to be abolished, it was done on the initiative of an Indian *man*, Ram Mohun Roy. When monogamy was to be emphasised as the one ideal of marriage, it was again from *a man*, Vidyasagar of Bengal, that the impulse came. In the East, it is not by selfish agitation, from within, that great reforms and extensions of privilege are brought about. It is by spontaneous effort, by gracious conferring of right from the other side. Or if indeed woman feel the pinch of some sharp necessity, some ill to be righted, is she not mother of man as well as of woman? Can she not whisper to her son, in his childhood, of the task to which she assigns him? And shall she not thus forge a weapon more powerful than any her own weak hands could wield? Such a woman was the mother of Pandit Iswar Chandra Vidyasagar and such was the inspiration that made him the woman's champion.

But one word there is to be said, of warning and direction to that young priesthood of learning, to whom this generation entrusts the problem we have been considering. Education can never be carried out by criticism or discouragement. Only he who sees the noblest thing in the taught can be an effective teacher. Only by the greatness of Indian life can we give a sense of the greatness of the world outside India. Only by the love of our own people can we learn the love of humanity—and only by a profound belief in the future of the Indian woman, can any man be made worthy to help in bringing that future about. Let the preacher of the New Learning be consecrated to the vision of one who resumes into herself the greatness of the whole Indian past. Let him hope and most earnestly pray that in this our time, in all our villages, we are to see women great even as Gandhari, faithful and brave as Savitri, holy and full of tenderness as Sita. Let the past be as wings unto the feet of the future. Let all that has been be as steps leading us up the mountain of what is yet to be. Let every Indian woman incarnate for us the whole spirit of the Mother and the culture and protection of the Homeland, *Bhumyâ Devi*! Goddess of the Homestead! *Bande Mâtaram*!

THE PROJECT OF THE RAMAKRISHNA SCHOOL FOR GIRLS.

The changes that have made Hindu education a Western problem completed themselves on the day when the declaration of the English Empire constituted India one of the countries of the modern world.

Till then, from a remote antiquity, the geographical isolation of the peninsula had been the opportunity for the evolution of a singularly perfect form of society. And the education of the individual, in adaptation to the structure of the community, was well understood.

There was full scope for all classes in competition with each other, a reasonable standard of comfort was attainable, and its definition generally accepted ; and the training which was to enable each man and woman to distribute the life-effort in due proportion between self and the social organism, had stood the test of time.

To-day, all this is changed. Ever since 1833 —when the East India Company's Charter was renewed, on condition that it ceased to carry on trade or manufacture, *i.e.*, ceased to foster and develop the industries and exports of that country as against home—India has stood out in the full current of world-commerce. And, like some ancient treasure that could not bear contact with the air, her own arts and wealth have crumbled to dust and been carried away by that stream. Her mysteriously lovely cottons are still to be bought in the land of Venice and Genoa, but they are "old, very old," nowadays. The one foreigner—Shah Jehan—who ever had the genius to see what might be done with the humble native crafts of mosaic and stone-cutting, and the munificence to do it, has had no successor. Aniline dyes are displacing the brilliant beauty of Oriental colors by the same sequence which is substituting English for Hindustani, and is tending to supplant the national treasures of Sanskrit, Hindi and the Dravidian tongues with the ephemeral literature of the nineteenth century of Europe.

Change is inevitable, even desirable ; but change need not mean decay. It is easy to see that India is still in the first shock of the modern catastrophe, not having yet realized even the elements of the new problem, much less having had time to evolve methods of solution. It is also plain that if the present pause in the national life is to prelude a process of restoration and development, rather than of disintegration, this can only be determined by some scheme of education which shall enable the people to conserve all that they have already achieved, while at the same time they adapt themselves to the needs of the new era.

The weaver's brain is not idle, as his shuttle flies to and fro on the loom, nor can he be set to this task without the co-operation of every part of his society. So, wherever characteristic industries exist, characteristic schemes of philosophy and cosmology, national epic cycles, bodies of speculation on abtruse subjects, and other accumulations of heightened individuality must also occur. This is pre-eminently the case in India, where contributions to mathematics, astronomy and other sciences have been of the greatest importance in the past, and are likely to be so again. Any education, therefore, that shall effectually meet the Indian need of self-adaptation must produce amongst other results, at least in the higher castes, an increased national self-consciousness, a sentiment of the vigour and responsibility of a young people, and an attitude of friendship and promise towards the other peoples of the world. To produce an Oriental in whom Orientalism had been intensified, while to it had been added the Western conception of the Cause of Humanity, of the Country, of the People as a whole, Western power of initiative and organization, Western energy and practicality—such an ideal should inspire our energy of culture in the East.

[It will be noted that this "conservation of national achievement" is not in any sense that of the antiquarian or the pedant who would strive, with a kind of refined selfishness, to retain the picturesqueness of things as they were.]

Towards such ends, the steps that have already been taken by the Government and others, where not actually misguided, have been merely preliminary. But all have been eagerly welcomed by the natives of the country. Their indebtedness to the educational missionary is something that the Indian people never forget, and from the Himalayas to Cape Comorin the names of great members of this profession, whether Protestant or Roman Catholic, are held in loving and grateful memory. To this day, every Hindu student at the University of Calcutta is required, by the tradition of his own people, to make a pilgrimage to the tomb of David Hare, the Scotsman, who a hundred years ago, founded the school that has since developed into the university ; died of cholera, caught in nursing a pupil through the illness ; was refused burial in christian ground, for his rationalistic tendencies ; and was finally carried on the heads of his own boys, and lovingly interred in a spot that stands to-day within the College Square. Every act of that little closing ceremony is eloquent to him who understands Hindu expression of passionate devotion and gratitude. It is the etiquette of India to entertain a guest according to his customs, whatever the trouble and cost ; and this delicate honor shines through the fact that burial —a thing abhorent to the Hindu—and not cremation, was the fate of David Hare. Then, again, actual contact with the dead was not deputed to those hirelings, who are amongst the lowest of the low, but was borne by high-caste youths themselves, at considerable personal risk. It is an inhuman thing to analyze an act of love, but we need to know the associations that lie behind this, in order to appreciate the demonstration at its true value. And further, reverence for tombs and relics being excessively Mohammedan, nothing could be more significant than this present habit of paying visits to Hare's tomb, of the depth of the impression made on the municipal imagination by this apostle of secular education.

Yet the days of David Hare, and many a great schoolmaster, were long over before the preliminary dispute—must the new code be dominated by the Eastern or Western classics?—could be decided by statesmen in the interests of a national form of instruction. It was settled at last, by Lord Dalhousie's adoption of Sir Charles Wood's scheme in 1854, by which existing native schools were recognized, inspected, and aided, while an acquaintance with the Vernacular in the first place, and English in the second, was made the great purpose of study. At the time, this was felt to be a wonderful solution of the question. But in the years since 1854 it has dawned upon all of us that education is not altogether a matter of words, nor even of information, and actual experience of its results has led the majority of English officials to be entirely dissatisfied with things as they are being done.

Yet in what direction changes are to be made is not clear either. The cost of teaching in Bengal is kept down rigorously to something like twenty-nine cents (or one shilling and two pence half-penny) per head per annum. Obviously, there is no margin here for expenditure on scientific laboratories, or manual training-schools!

On the other hand, in a population so large as three hundred millions, the course once entered on can never be retracted, though it may be modified in direction, and results have to be reckoned with, however unexpected, in kind. The Unification of India, as Sir William Hunter pointed out, through the half-penny post, cheap railway travel and the popularity of English education, is one of the least foreseen of these. It will readily be understood how dangerous in many ways to the best interests, alike of rulers and ruled, is such unification, reached, as it is apt to be, through the cheap and vapid Europeanism of mere reading.

Thus far, all that has been said applies to boys equally with girls. When we come to consider the latter, however, as a separate problem, we are met by new considerations.

Oriental women are much more tenacious of custom, and of the old form of training, than the men. Like women of the old regime in other countries, they are all required to marry —without, in their case, the alternative of the protection of the Church—and that early. Economic causes have postponed the usual age of this solemn betrothal nowadays, to as late as twelve years. The period between the ceremony and the day of entering the mother-in-law's household, at about the age of fourteen, is supposed to be divided by the little bride in visits alternately to the old home and the new.

Should the husband die during these years, the girl is as much a widow as if she had already taken up her abode with him, and social honor makes re-marriage equally impossible. Cases of this kind constitute the class known as "child widows." Their lives henceforth become those of nuns. They are expected to embody a specially high ideal of austerity and devotion. But in return for this they meet with the approval and respect of all about them, and not—as has so mistakenly been supposed—with hatred and contempt.

If all goes happily, however, the bride at twelve becomes a wife at fourteen, and passes into a position of duty and responsibility in the home of her husband's mother. Up to this time she has been a petted and indulged child. [The over-tenderness of the Hindu family for the little daughters who are to leave them so early, is a fruitful source of difficulty in the school room.] At this period, all that might strictly be called education begins for her, and the wonderful dignity and savoir-faire of the Hindu woman's bearing is a sure witness to the training of the careful mother-in-law.

Translated into terms of deeper simplicity and poverty, we have the Bower of the old Feudal castle represented in the women's apartments of a Hindu home to-day. It is not tapestries and embroideries that employ our maidens, indeed, but the more homely matters of house-cleaning and cooking, the milking of the family-cow, and the bringing-up of children. There are likely to be many girls of an age, in the household, as wives of brothers and cousins, and their relationship to the older ladies of the family culminates in the deference paid to "the mother," who is in her turn mother or wife of the chief of kin. Certainly no old poem or romance was ever perused more eagerly by the fair dames of the days of chivalry than are the Indian Epics and Puranas within the Zenana. Even the parties of strolling minstrels who sang and acted in the Castle-hall have their parallel, for in the spring evenings it often happens that a Ramayana-party is given, and seated behind screens on the courtyard verandah, where they can see without being seen, the ladies listen to the ever-old and ever-new story of the wanderings of Sita and Rama in the forest.

Such innocent pleasures, however, are growing less frequent, for the modest means that were necessary to secure them are yearly diminishing. The men of the Indian higher classes are sinking into a race of cheap English clerks, and are becoming more and more incapable of supporting their numerous dependents. New activities, calling for enterprise and power of combination will have to be opened up by them, if this state of things is to be retrieved. And, in such an epoch of reconstruction, the sympathy and co-operation of the women will be absolutely necessary as a social force.

It is obvious that their present education is largely a discipline rather than a development. Yet it has not altogether precluded the appearance of great individuals. Witness, amongst many others, that widowed Rani of Jhansi, who emerged from her seclusion in the days of the Mutiny, to make proclamations, issue a new coinage, cast cannon, and finally to die in battle with us, at the head of her own troops.

Sporadic instances of this kind nevertheless, serve rather to show the virility of a race than to prove the rightness of a system of training. It is undeniable that if we could add to the present lives of Indian women, larger scope for individuality, a larger social potentiality and some power of economic redress, without adverse criticism, direct or indirect, of present institutions, we should achieve something of which there is dire necessity.

Now, thanks to the efforts of Christian missionaries and others, two kinds of education are within reach of some—the three R's as taught in the primary school and a university degree. As the orthodox usually seclude their daughters after marriage, the school-course in their case, has to end at ten or twelve. In the case of Christians, the Brahmo Samaj and Parsis degrees are quite commonly carried off by women! But taking these, and all similar instances into consideration, the total number of girls in Bengal who receive formal instruction is only six and a half per cent. of the population. And Bengal is said to be in this respect the most advanced province.

There is, therefore, a great need. We are also agreed in some measure as to the character of the answer. The question that remains is, How and where can we make a beginning in offering to Indian women an education that shall mean development adapted to the actual needs of their actual lives?

It is after careful study and consideration of such facts as these that the project of the Ramakrishna School for Girls has been formed.

We intend, if we succeed in acquiring means,

to buy a house and piece of land on the banks of the Ganges, near Calcutta, and there to take in some twenty widows and twenty orphan girls —the whole community to be under the guidance and authority of that SARADA DEVI, whose name has been lately introduced to the world by Professor Max Muller in his "Life and sayings of Ramakrishna."

It is further proposed to add to this establishment a scholastic institution in which the best manual training can be given.

The school course is to be founded on the Kinder-garten, and is to include the English and Bengali languages and literature, elementary mathematics very thoroughly taught, some elementary science very thoroughly taught, and handicrafts, with a special bearing on the revival of the old Indian industries. The immediate justification of the last subject would lie in enabling every pupil to earn her own living, without leaving her home, by a pursuit which should be wholly ennobling.

But the school is to have a second function. The widows—whom we may reckon as from eighteen to twenty years of age—are not only to be useful in giving the true Hindu background and home-life, but amongst them we look to organize two or three industries for which promising markets can be opened up in England, India, and America. Amongst these, the making of native jams, pickles and chutneys, is to be included.

Supposing our effort to be in every way successful—supposing, above all, that it approves itself to Hindu society as in no sense *denationalizing*—it will probably be possible slightly to defer the day on which we ask each child to choose for herself the life of marriage or of consecrated national service. For those who choose the first, we shall hope to provide ways and means that are entirely creditable. With any who may prefer to devote their lives to unremitting toil on behalf of their country and her womanhood, we shall expect, after an extended education, and using the older women as guards and protectors, to start new Ramakrishna schools in other centres.

And, let me say, in conclusion, that I trust I am seeking to divert no energy or gift from the near duty to the far. In these days of international commerce and finance, we are surely realizing that only World-Service is true Home-Service. Already, we seem to be answering Walt Whitman's sublime question in the affirmative—

"Are all nations communing? Is there going to be but one heart to the globe?"

SOME QUESTIONS ANSWERED BY SISTER NIVEDITA, IN THE WEST, IN CONNECTION WITH THE FOREGOING.

1.—What is your purpose in establishing your school in India?

ANS.—To give *Education* [not instruction merely] to orthodox Hindu girls, in a form that is suited to the needs of the country. [I recognize that if any Indian institutions are faulty it is the right of the Indian people themselves to change them. We may only aim to produce ripe judgment and power of action. Also, I consider that we should confer a direct benefit on any Indian woman whom we could enable to earn her own living, without loss of social honor.]

2.—What class of women are they to teach?

ANS.—Unfortunately our first efforts must be directed to the higher classes. Eventually, I hope to reach all, partly through Hindu girls who will be eager to specialize in various social directions.

3.—Are they not educational schools only?

ANS.—What does this mean? I do not seek to convert any one to Christianity.
Neither any Christian to anything else.
Neither any Mohammedan to Hinduism or Christianity.

Is this an answer?

4.—What are they to teach?

ANS.—1, 2—Bengali and English language and literature.

3—Elementary mathematics (very thoroughly).

4—(some one) Elementary Science (very thoroughly).

5—MANUAL TRAINING, beginning in the kindergarten and rising to the point of reviving old Indian industries and arts later on.

No. 5 is the backbone of the plan.

5.—Is not your idea a humanitarian one?

To help the helpless and needy regardless of creed?

And to teach no creed?

ANS.—I hope so.

But I would like to teach every one the greatest respect for everyone else's creed!

Perhaps no one needs *this* virtue as we ourselves do. In India, my friends love me for my love love of Christianity, and talk with me about it for hours together. Can we not show like sweetness and courtesy?

April 2nd, 1900.

SUGGESTIONS FOR THE INDIAN VIVEKANANDA SOCIETIES.

Throughout the length and breadth of India, and especially perhaps in the Southern Presidency, one comes upon towns and villages possessing Vivekananda Societies. A group of students, fired by the glorious name, band themselves together with a vague idea of doing something to justify its adoption and then turn round to enquire—what?

What shall be the main duty of Vivekananda Societies?

In a Western country, the answer would be, Work!

In Protestant lands, there would perhaps be an effort to work and live in the city slums, to assist in local sanitation, to carry on attempts at manual education,—such as wood-carving, or metal and glass work,—or athletic training, or even to organise amusements only, amongst those who were socially lower and less fortunate than the Vivekananda boys themselves.

In Catholic countries, the seven corporal works of mercy [feeding the hungry, giving drink to the thirsty, clothing the naked, nursing the sick, visiting prisoners, harbouring the harbourless, burying the dead], would be the natural expression of the energy of these societies, which would become in effect minor associations of some great religious order, relating themselves to the Order of Ramakrishna, for instance, as their Third Orders are related to the Franciscans and Dominicans, or as, amongst women, the Filles de Marie are affiliated to the Society of Jesus.

But India falls under neither of these headings.

She resembles the catholic country, indeed, rather than the Protestant, but with this difference—that the virtues which the Church is striving to promulgate, she has long ago assimilated, and expresses in the natural course of her social life. To feed the hungry and give drink to the thirsty, outside their own families, is part of the everyday routine of Eastern households. Bestowal of money or clothing on those who need is a duty regularly distributed amongst the wealthy. For roadside mercies we have only to note the *dharmashâlâs* outside each village, the bathing-ghats on the river-banks, and the stone posts and lintels that enable the coolie to re-adjust his burden along every highway of the South. And with regard to the rite that corresponds to burial, only Indian lads themselves know how common it is for high-caste boys to undertake the bearing of the dead to the burning-ghat by way of honourable assistance to the poor. Asia is the Mother of Religions, simply and solely because she practises as obvious social functions those virtues that Southern Europe would be glad to ignore, save for ecclesiastical pressure, and that Northern Europe has been driven to regiment, as functions of state and township, in the winter of an extreme ungraciousness.

So it would be carrying coals to Newcastle, as we say in England, if the name of our great *Guru* were to represent merely an effort like this,—to religionise the already religious. What then of the first method of action? Why should not that be ours? Do we in India not require, as much as England or America, a greater equalising of conditions? the revival and extension of the arts and crafts? the universalising of athletics, especially in their old Indian forms of wrestling, club-whirling and stick-play, though not these to the exclusion of the modern cricket, football, tennis, drilling? the spread of technical industries? more sympathy and co-operation in their leisure between caste and caste?

Alas, we need all these things! Indeed it might be urged that the Swami's name represents, more than anything else, a transition from the one period, as it were, to the other, a transition which was already inevitable, but which has been rendered secure and non-disruptive by the fact that he combined in his single person the strength of both the phases of society. For, his was that superconsciousness that alone seals the mission of the supreme religious teacher in theocratic civilisations and at the same time, he was full of the fearlessness and hope, the national *shraddhâ* and devotion to the people which must form the characteristics of those who are to re-make India. On the other hand, we must not forget that the form of work which we are considering is a free growth out of modern conditions of labour and education in Western lands. The formation of natural history clubs, of town-boys and villagers, to hunt for microscope-specimens on Sundays under the direction of some advanced student, would be to the full as delightful and desirable in India as in England. But, obviously, it could only be done by Indians with Indians and for Indians. Read the *Life of Charles Kingsley* or read even Mrs. Humphrey Ward's pleasant novel *Robert Elsmere*, and realise the overflow of the sense of union with people and soil, the overflow of strength and gladness that speaks in what may be called this beautiful, "vicarage-life" of England, so like the more modern University Settlement ideal. It is to be feared that without similar antecedents to make them untrammelled and spontaneous, efforts like these for our Vivekananda Societies would be at this moment merely parasitic and imitative. That the boys should devote themselves heart and soul to the creating of a great love of the People is what we need ; but that that love should be forced into a premature expression of itself in forms natural only to the foreigner, would surely be base and misguided.

But a more obvious objection to the adoption of such programmes by the Vivekananda Societies is the practical difficulty to be encountered in carrying them out. The members are for the most part students in schools and colleges. Their future depends on the passing of specified examinations at specified times, and so little are these ordeals related to the actual life of the country and the family that in order to be successful a boy must devote his whole time and attention to the matter suppressing himself completely, from eleven to twenty-one years of age. Amongst Indian men again, there are few who can live unto themselves. Almost all our youths are struggling with their school books, not for their own sakes, but in order to maintain their families, to lift the burden of aged parents, or widowed sisters, at as early an age as possible. It would rarely be practicable therefore for them, even had they the necessary wealth, to undertake, as mere leisure work, the extended activities of a London Toynbee Hall, or a Chicago Hull House, during their student-years.

Some kind of attempt to extend their own knowledge and that of the women of their households, on such subjects as sanitation, the properties of food, and the nursing of the sick, there might well be indeed. Other efforts to promote physical exercise in the old forms—so productive of special skill and muscularity—and in the new forms. so conducive to power of co-operation and organisation, there ought also to be. That these efforts should have a direct bearing further, on the welfare of the lower castes, is beyond doubt. Our best interests are involved in such an attitude.

But many of the Vivekananda Societies may feel that definite work for these ends is outside their present scope ; that the true task of a student is study ; that therefore the wisest course they can propose to themselves is a constant reading of the books of the Swami Vivekananda, with a view to assimilating his thought and expressing it later in their own lives. Those who adopt this method are likely to encounter two difficulties.

In the first place, they will be apt to neglect the forest for the trees. In reading the *works* of Vivekananda, they are liable to forget that behind all his books, all his utterances, stands the man himself, different from each, only partially expressed through the whole mass. But it is this man-himself that they really need to understand and appropriate ; his triumph that they require to realise ; his ringing cheer of hope and defiance that they should strive to make their own.

The second difficulty before the students is still more serious. There is a danger of turning the Swami's books into a new bondage, by treating every word of the text as sacred, and reading and re-reading constantly, till the brain is dazed and the ears are deafened and we lose all chance of understanding, even as the Christian child loses the beauty of the English Bible, or the Temple-Brahmin forgets the thrill of the Salutations. The Swami himself was a great incarration of freedom. To sit in his presence was to experience an emancipation.

He was nothing, if not a breaker of bondage. How then can a Vivekananda Society, in faithfulness to him, undertake to fasten handcuffs upon the mind? Is it not clear that only when our own thought is first active can we understand the value of his opinions and decisions? People who are already much troubled by questions about caste are prepared to appreciate his utterances on this subject in the Six Madras Lectures. Boys who are in love with their own land, and longing to conceive of her as a unity, will revel in the detailed knowledge and the dazzling succession of pictures contained in the Reply to the Madras Address. Only those who have themselves begun to enquire what Hinduism is, and who are baffled by the vastness of the enquiry the problem presents, will be in a position to comprehend the great speech at Chicago.

But, it will be asked, how are we then to get at the true significance of the Swami's utterances as a whole? Obviously, we must first tackle the questions that he tackled. In this way, our very difficulties will help us to understand his meaning. It has been well said that the true disciple is he who is caught heart and soul by the idea that caught his master, and proceeds to work it out, in ways that the master never thought of and might not even have approved. What was the idea that caught Vivekananda? Is it not plain enough for him that runs to read? He saw before him a great Indian nationality, young, vigorous, fully the equal of any nationality on the face of the earth. To him, this common nationality—conscious of its own powers, and forcing their recognition on others, moving freely forward to its own goal in all worlds, intellectual, material, social, occupational—was that "firm establishment of the national righteousness (*dharma*)" for which those who love him believe undoubtingly that he was born.

But, it will be said, it was easy for the Swami to conceive of an Indian nationality. He was a great traveller. On the one hand, he knew India from end to end. On the other, he had seen most of the countries of the world. And nothing teaches like contrast. This argument is true, and points to the fact that one of the great duties of Vivekananda Societies should be the revival of the enthusiasm for pilgrimages. It is not Kedar Nath alone that we see by going there. How much do we not learn of India! How deep do we not go into the passion of the race for their beautiful Himalayas! How much may we not add to our power of thought and feeling by a single visit to Benares Is not the definite and living knowledge of him who has performed the four great *tirthas* well worth having?

It is of course quite impossible for large numbers of our youths to go abroad, in order to awaken their own sense of home-characteristics. Nor would it, we may add, in the majority of cases be of the least use. Very few observers are competent to avail themselves of the extended opportunities of foreign travel, for in this field, above all, it is true that a man sees only what his mind has brought the power of seeing. The real question is, How can we educate ourselves to *understand* the contrasts and affinities between India and other countries?

One great means lies in the cultivation of the historical sense. "Every man," says Emerson, "is a quotation from all his ancestors." Every moment, in like manner, is a compendium of the whole past. We need not devote ourselves to the history of India alone, or even chiefly. To know this, will become an imperious hunger in us, in proportion as our conception of the national process in other lands grows clearer.

Why not take the *Stories of the Nations* series of text books, and study the tale of ancient

Chaldæa, Assyria, Egypt? Why not trace out the origin and development of Islam, pondering over its immense struggles in Syria, in Spain, and around Constantinople? Why not interest ourselves in Persia, in Venice, in the history of the Crusades, in ancient Greece, if we can find opportunity not omitting China and Japan.

But we could go even deeper than these things, and study the nature of human societies and commonwealths themselves. Spencer's *Study of Sociology*, in the International Science Series, is a fine starting-point. It gives clear, definite lines of self-culture, which should be as the words of the Vedas to the earnest student. There are multitudes of works on Sociology, on Primitive Man, and on allied subjects, by many modern writers, such as Spencer, Lubbock, Tylor, Fiske, Clodd, and others, but most of the books of the first-named writer are too special for the purpose we are considering. Very important to the Hindu reader, by reason of the pride and confidence it inspires in his own faith, is Draper's *Conflict of the Religious and Scientific Spirits*,—a work on a merely European subject. Frederic Harrison's *Meaning of History*, and *Congreve's International Policy* are also specially commendable, though the extraordinary ignorance of the East which they manifest should be rather as provocation than as authority to Indian boys. And just as the enquiry into matters of orthodox interest may fitly end with an appeal to the Swami Vivekananda's books, to see what they happen to say on the subject, so this historical and sociological research has always, for India, a supreme court of appeal, in the Charge of Bhishma to Judhisthira in the Shanti Parva of the *Mahabharata*. Here we have the utmost of royal insight and wisdom concentrated upon the question of national well-being, and every student before he studies, should sit self-crowned, bearing the cares and responsibilities of kings amongst kings, that he may understand in all their actuality these words of the Indian sovereigns of old.

It is well-known however that all great ages dawn with a mighty wave of hero-worship. The enthusiasm that leads to the formation of the Vivekananda Societies themselves is an instance of this. History cannot be entirely philosophical. Let us plunge madly into the worship of great characters. Nothing could be more akin to the Swami Vivekananda's own spirit. He would spend hours in talk of Buddha or Sita or S. Francis or even perhaps of some great personage living at the moment in a foreign land. And he would throw himself into the very soul of the hero, never failing to throw the light of some new and startling interpretation upon character and narrative.

Why then should the Vivekananda Societies not get given members to discover all that is possible about, for instance, Akbar, or Rani Ahalya Bai, Protap Singh of Chittore, the *Gurus* of the Sikhs, or Pericles, Saladin, Joan of Arc, George Washington, and then read papers, embodying their study? Or again, some special crisis in the story of a people might be worked up, Italy from 1820 to 1860, Japan before and after 1867, the French Revolution, the ancient struggle of the Greek against the Persian. These, as has been well said, are the *nodes of history.* They are a national education in themselves.

A useful method of work will be found to be that of common discussion. It is only by inducing the boys to study, argue, and think out for themselves the subjects and questions proposed that we can reach a free and living knowledge. At the end of an informal conversation or formal debate, as the case may be, passages might be read from the Swami's other books, by way of ascertaining some authoritative verdict. In some such way we might hope to be secure from danger of deadening the intelligence, and degrading the opinion of the *Guru*, by making of it a new bondage.

For he is not the greatest teacher who can tell us most, but he who leads us to ask the deepest questions. Let us then prepare ourselves to ask questions, and as we return to the Swami's own works after each month or six weeks of such intellectual excursions, we may rest assured that we shall find them more and more luminous, till at last his whole personality stands revealed to us, because we have learnt to love even as he loved, to hope as he hoped, and to believe as he believed.

A NOTE ON HISTORICAL RESEARCH.

1. In all that you do, be dominated by the moral aim. Remember that Truth, in its fulness, is revealed, not only through the intellect, but also through the heart, and the will. Never rest content, therefore, with a realisation which is purely mental. And never forget that every act of our lives is a necessary sacrifice to knowledge, that a man who consciously chooses a mean or ignoble course *cannot* long continue to be a pioneer in the march of his fellows onwards. Only if we are always striving, in every way for the highest that is attainable can we actually achieve anything at all in any path.

It has been said that "the great scientific discoveries are great social events." This is true of all advances in learning. We labour, even to win truth, not on behalf of Self, but on behalf of man and the fruits of our labour are to be given to man, not selfishly enjoyed. Better a low attainment generously shared, than a high vision seen by oneself alone. Better, because more finally effective to the advance of knowledge The result of the struggle of the individual in our generation ought to be the starting-point of the race in the next.

2. Never be contented with the ideas and the wisdom which are gathered in the study. We are bodies as well as minds. We have other senses and other faculties, besides those of language. We have limbs as well as brains. Use the body. Use all the senses, use even the limbs in the pursuit of truth. That which is learned, not only with the mind, by means of manuscripts and books, but also through the eyes and the touch, by travel and by work, is really known. Therefore, if you want to understand India, visit the great historic centres of each age. Turn over the earth and stroke the chiselled stones, with your own hands, walk to the sight that you want to see, if possible, rather than ride. Ride rather than drive. *Stand* in the spot, where an event happened, even if no trace of its occurrence is still visible. If you desire to understand a religious idea, reproduce as perfectly as you can, in every detail, the daily life of the man to whom it came, or the race to which it was familiar. To understand the Buddhist *Bhikku,* go out and beg. To understand Aurangzebe, sit in the mosquê at Delhi, and pray there the prayers of the Mohammedan.

Or, if social formations are your study, be sure to *work*, to *experiment*, as well as to learn. Verify each truth, test each idea, that comes to you. Whatever you seek, bend every faculty on its achievement. What you believe, make yourself to it as dough kneaded by the baker, as clay worked by the potter, as the channel to the water of the river. Spurn ease. Never rest content. Make thought into sensation ; sensation into experience ; experience into knowledge. Let knowledge become character. Glory in suffering. By what your work costs *you*, you may know its possible value to the world.

3. Never forget the future. "By means of the past to understand the present, *for the conquest of the future.*" Let this be your motto. Knowledge without a purpose is mere pedantry. Yet at the same time, the intrusion of self-interest upon the pursuit of knowledge, must be turned aside, as with the flaming sword. Purpose, moral purpose, others-regarding purpose is the very antithesis of self-interest. Refuse to be drawn into personal, social, or doctrinal disputes. Release the energy that belongs to these worlds, and let it find a higher function, in aiding you to your self-chosen goal.

4. And now comes the question of the scope of your work, the question of what you

are actually to do. On two points I know you to be clear,—first, you are determined, whatever you do, through it to serve the Indian Nationality ; and second, you know that to do this, you must make yourself a world-authority in that particular branch of work. On these two points, therefore, I do not need to dwell. With regard to the actual field of labour, it has long, I think, been determined amongst us that India's assimilation of the modern spirit may be divided into three elements, which She has not only to grasp but also to democratise. These are: Modern Science ; Indian History ; and the World-Sense or Geography,—Synthetic Geography.

5. Now in whichever of these you choose your own task, most of your intellectual *pleasure* must come from the others. If you were a worker in Science, you might read a good deal of History, in interesting forms, as recreation. And so on. One of the modes by which a line of high research becomes democratised is just this. The historical epoch, for instance, that is opened up by the scholar is immediately appropriated and clothed with flesh, by the novelist, the poet and the dramatist. Scott's novels have been one of the chief factors in the creation of the modern spirit. And you do not

need to be told what poetry has done for the popularising of Buddhist research amongst the English-speaking peoples.

6. But whatever you do, plunge into it heart and soul. Believe that, in a sense, it alone,—this modern form of knowledge, young though it be,—*is true*. Carry into it no prepossessions, no prejudices. Do not try, through it, to prove that your ancestors understood all things, but manfully determine to add its mastery to the intellectual realm of your ancestor's descendants. I see this vice on all hands. People imagine that it is "national" to reply when told something new that ought to thrill them through and through, "Ah yes, I am familiar with that in Sanskrit, or from the *Mahabharata*, or from the sayings of such and such a *Sadhu*." And there their thought ends. This is pure idleness and irreverence. Such recognition kills thought, and coffins it: it offers it no home in which to dwell, no garden in which to grow! The man who would conquer new realms intellectually must never look back except to find tools. The man who would see truth face to face must first wash his eyes in dew, unused by human kind. Afterwards, when the task is done, when you come home laden with your spoils, you may perform the great

sacrifice of reverence. You may tally this and that, amongst your own discoveries, with this and that amongst the utterances of the forefathers, and find, in an ecstacy of reconciliation, that you have gone by the same road as they, only calling the milestones by different names. But, to-day, set your face sternly towards the tabulation of *difference*, towards the new, the strange, the unproven, and undreamt, you will prove yourself the true son of your father, not by wearing garments of their fashions but by living their life, by fighting with their strength. Concentration and renunciation are the true differentiæ of the Hindu mind, not certain subjects of study, or a pre-occupation with Sanskrit.

7. And now, as to the subject itself. Already you have progressed in the direction of History and Indian Economics. It is to be supposed therefore that your work itself will be somewhere in this region. But side by side with your own specialism—in which you will faithfully do, with your trained habits, what Professor Jadu Nath Sarkar calls "spade-work"—do not forget to interest yourself in subjects as a whole. If you take up Geography, read History for recreation, but be a great geographer, like Reclus. If you take up History do not forget to read Reclus' Universal Geography, and every

other synthetic work that you can find. The mind seeks energy by reposing in synthesis or unity, and uses the energy so acquired, in analytical or specialistic fields. Again if Indian History be your work of research, read the finest European treatises on Western History. They may not always be valuable for their facts, but they are priceless for their methods. Read Buckle and Lecky as well as Gibbon. And read the great Frenchmen if you can. It is said that Bossuet's short work on the movement of History, written for a Dauphin of France, was the spark that set the soul of Napoleon on fire. I have not yet read it but I hope to do so. I hope also to read Condorcet and Lamartine, and more than I have yet done of Michelet. About Comte, I feel unable to advise you. I believe fully that his has been the greatest mind ever devoted to History. But whether his treatment of the subject is as valuable as his conclusions, I am unable to tell you ; for my own part, I have hitherto only been able to grasp a little bit at a time, and with regard to the thousands of questions that are in my mind, I cannot even tell whether he has given definite answers to them or not. Yet the two books that I have lent you, by an English Positivist,—"The Meaning of History"—and "The New Calendar of Great Men,"

—seem to me, though very popular yet extremely profound. As I have already pointed out to you, the short essays with which each division of the latter book is introduced, and the connectedness of the treatment of each life with others, are to my mind worth their weight in gold.

In Indian History, such a point of view is conspicuous by its absence. Some writers are interested in Buddhist India (if indeed we have any right to employ such a term) and some in various stages of Mahratta or Sikh or Indo-Islamic History, or what not. But who has caught the palpitation of the *Indian* heart-beat through one and all of these? It is *India* that makes Indian History glorious. It is *India* that makes the whole joy of the Indian places. I felt this when I was at Rajgir, and saw so plainly, shining through the Buddhist period, the outline and colour of an earlier India still,—the *India* of the *Mahabharata.* And the other day amongst the ruins at Sanchi, when a lady who had been in Egypt turned and said to me, "If you think so much of 2,000 years what would you think of 4,000?" I said "I care nothing for 2,000! Even Sanchi is but a heap of stones. *But this strength is in the Indian people still!*"

Are you the man who can catch this truth,

and justify it before the whole world by the mingling of stern scholarship, with poetic warmth? Better still, are you the man who can make India herself feel it? An Upanishad of the National History would make eternal foundations for the Indian Nationality, in the Indian heart, the only world in which the nationality can be built enduringly. Or do you lean rather to the economic side of your studies? If so, do not allow yourself to become a mère specialist on statistics, and still more earnestly guard yourself against being the one person in the world who knows all that is to be known about India's grievances, and knows nothing else. Every country and every community in the world has grievances, and grievances against certain definite other persons and communities also. To *think* of our mistakes and weaknesses as our grievances against another, is to postpone indefinitely the day of setting them right. The active, the aggressive, attitude is quite different. Accepting the past—and if you wish to be proud of some of your ancestor's deeds, you must be calmly prepared to suffer for others. The law of opposites will hold here, as elsewhere!—the question is, what is to be done next? Even the science of economics may be made moral, may be made constructive. The doctrine that man always does what pays him, is vulgar nonsense. In fact the highest men are rather attracted to the opposite extreme, of doing always what does *not* pay.

Ruskin, Wicksteed and the Fabians, amongst English writers, may help one to a true view-point for economics, for these have felt the wholeness of human interests, through the specialism. For the technology of the subject, you must read many books. But the morality and wholesomeness of human love, in it, you will share with very few, and those nearly always representatives of some *cult* or other, which teaches the love and service, instead of the exploiting and extermination, of human beings, as the highest and most permanent joy of man. There is however a third subject which you might take up, and feed from both your studies, of Indian History and Indian Economics. I allude to *Sociology,* or the Study of Society. This term was the creation of Comte, but was popularised by Herbert Spencer, a very different person. Spencer and a host of other writers have gone into the subject, through the study of *Customs,* in which there can be little doubt that the history of society is chiefly written. Comte regarded it rather from the point of view of an organism having a meaning, a responsibility and a destiny. He saw the whole spirituality of man in every human being of every human race! And many writers have attempted to work out theories of society, by comparing those of men with those of ants and bees and so on. King of modern sociologists is perhaps Kropotkin, with his book on *Mutual Aid* published by Heinemann, in which he works out the idea that mutual aid, co-operation, self-organisation, have been much stronger factors than the competition of fellows, in the evolution of the higher forms of life and in the determining of success for the community.

Now this is surely a line of thought and research which is *most* important to the question of Nationality. In my own opinion, we are entering here on a new period in which *Mutual Aid, Co-operation, Self-organisation,* is to be the motto, and we want, not only determined workers, but also great leaders, equipped with all the knowledge that is to be had, and therefore capable of leading us in thought. Is it true that an industrial society represents the highest social formation? If so, is it equally true that it is always based upon an antecedent military? "From the military, through the active, to the industrial," some one said to me the other day.

We stand here on the verge of great questions. Yet one thing would seem clear—only a people who are capable of industrialism, are capable of anything else. If the beginning determines the end, clearly the end also determines the beginning; the struggle to become fully industrialised is as high as the highest struggle that there is.

Even to write the History of India, even to set down clearly the problems which that history involves, I have long felt that we must first have experts in sociology,—men who can at a glance assign to a social group its possible age in pre-historic chronology. We want after that, and combined with it, those to whom the History of the early Asiatic Empires,—Chaldean, Assyrian, Tartar, Pelasgian, Egyptian, Phoenician,—is an open book. And, lastly, we want those who are competent to look out upon the future and determine towards what goal, by what line upon the traceless ocean, the great ship of national well-being is to be navigated.

Are you to be a solitary student? Or are you one of those most happy and fruitful workers who can call about them fellow-captains and fellow-crewsmen to toil along the same lines and exchange the results of thought?

A NOTE ON CO-OPERATION.

As to what you can read. First, for what *part* of the national work do you wish to train yourself? I believe, if rightly carried on, India is now entering on a period in which her motto is to be—"Mutual Aid: Self-organisation: Co-operation."

If you will look into the matter you will see that most cases of oppression and corruption—where the advantage of numbers is so uniformly on one side, as here—could be met by *Organisation.* It is more difficult to do wrong to ten thousand men who stand solid and are intelligent, than to an isolated and illiterate person. Take the case of clerks in offices, of Government servants, railway servants, rate payers, peasants. Much could be done amongst all these classes by simple enrolment and united action. But everything depends on such cases on the organiser, who is usually the Secretary. Do you care to do such work as this? It is not merely for self-protection that the organ could be used, but for obtaining credit, tools, knowledge, co-operation and mutual aid of many kinds.

If this is the branch which you are to take up, you will find that the subject has a history and a literature of its own. Read up *Co-operation* in the Encyclopædia Britannica. * * Read *Mutual Aid*, a scientific work, by Kropotkin, published by Heinemann. Study the history of Trade Unions. Study the history of Co-operation in Denmark. And study particularly the history of small countries, Norway, Sweden, the Hanseatic League, Motley's Rise of the Dutch Republic, etc. Make a small society for reading and discussing these subjects. Indeed do this in any case. Share your own knowledge, and co-operate in extending and deepening it. Above all, think things out, and put your thought into practice, learning from your own mistakes. Organise a single group of people for some definite aim, and see how you get on. Organise a class for, say, legal aid. That ought not to be difficult. But I think it would be a better experiment to make than organising for a charity, an enterprise which we are all accustomed to attempting and failing in. Organise for a united struggle of some kind, against something definite.

Or do you want to specialise in politics? In that case you must study the Economic History of India,—and the Congress publications, together with the books of Dutt, Digby, Naoroji, P. C. Ray and others, with the speeches of Ranade, Gokhale, and so on, will be your best fare.

Or is it *India*? In that case, work at History and do not neglect the History and Geography of other countries besides your own. For remember, it is the national sense *in* the world-sense that we have to achieve. The structure of human society,—Spencer, Tylor, Clodd, Lubbock and others ; the history of Early Empires, —Assyria, Chaldea, China, Persia, Egypt, Greece, etc., and for India,—Tilak's two books, Fergusson's Architecture, Cunningham's Ancient India, and other books. M'Crindle's collections. Archæological survey reports etc., etc., etc. In this kind of reading, constantly reinforced by pilgrimages to the places of which you read as far as possible—you can find the materials for a history yet to be written.

Or will you serve the great cause through the Industrial Revival? In that case all that helps for co-operation should help you. And a different class of work is wanted.

Or do you care to undertake the work of getting modern knowledge written up in the vernaculars? 'What books have you in your own vernacular, in which *women* can read

History? If you worked at this, in your own language, you would need helpers, an army of them. And then, again, you would want the courage that is born of feeling that others were carrying out the same idea in other languages.

For this, we would need the heroic devotion of thousands, of our choicest graduates the country over, each choosing his own subject, and filling up a single space in your great roll. There is nothing that so much needs doing. Nothing that would bring more illumination with it. Here is a case of co-operation. Each man would give only a few hours of leisure daily. The rest of his time he would be earning his bread. Do you see?

But there are other causes. There is physical training, for example. This is much needed. And so on and so on.

In any case read everything you can lay hands on, by Frederick Harrison. His books are expensive, but worth their weight in gold. They are published by Macmillan.

THE PLACE OF THE KINDER-GARTEN IN INDIAN SCHOOLS.

I.

The beautiful word *Kinder-garten*—garden of children—is known to-day throughout the world. Unfortunately, the truths that brought it into being, are not equally familiar, or equally apprehended. The ideal child-garden would seem to be the home, with the mother as the gardener. And if all mothers understood the development of man, and knew how to make the most of their flower-world, this would undoubtedly be the truest and noblest school for childhood. Nay, so far goes instinct, and so much greater is feeling than learnedness, that a babe were better abandoned to the loving care of the simplest mother, than to the harsh knowledge of a soured and withered teacher. But as facts stand, the mother needs the teacher's knowledge of the aim subserved, while undoubtedly the teacher needs the mother's lovingness and care.

Great men work out knowledge, and give it to the community. Thus each civilisation becomes distinguished by its characteristic institutions. Nothing could be more perfect educationally than the *bratas* which Hindu society has preserved and hands to its children in each generation, as first lessons in worship, so in the practice of social relationships, or in manners. Some of these *bratas*—like that which teaches the service of the cow, or the sowing of seeds, or some which seem to set out on the elements of geography and astronomy—have an air of desiring to impart what we now distinguish as secular knowledge. They appear, in fact, like surviving fragments of an old educational scheme. But for the most part, they constitute a training in religious ideas and religious feelings. As such, their perfection is startling. They combine practice, story, game, and object, with a precision that no Indian can appreciate or enjoy as can the European familiar with modern educational speculation. India has, in these, done on the religious and social plane, what Europe is trying, in the Kinder-garten, to do on the scientific. When we have understood the *bratas*, we cease to wonder at the delicate grace and passivity of the Oriental woman. Where a child has learnt to stand before a plant, asking permission mentally to cut its blossoms, how shall the acts of the woman be rude or ill-considered? "O Tulasi, beloved of Vishnu," says the little maiden, about to gather the basil-leaves for worship, "grant me the blessing to take you to His feet!" and only after a pause does she begin to pluck.

The Kinder-garten lessons of Europe, then, might be described as a series of *bratas*, designed to launch the child's mind on a knowledge of science. Like the religious *bratas* of India, they deal, in the first place, directly with the concrete objects. These objects are introduced by means of stories. In the course of the lesson, or "play"—or *brata*, as it might be called,—some definite act is performed repeatedly. And finally, in the highly-perfected lesson the result is a game, consisting of a song set to music, to be sung by the children, henceforth, in action. These four parts, then, story, object, action and the resultant game, make up the typical child-garden exercise. By their means, the mind of the learner is made to go through a definite sequence of experiences, on which a higher sequence may be constructed later. These four elements make up the child-world as a whole and in its parts. And the problem of child-education is so to use the typical *brata* as to initiate by its means in the learner, an ordered consciousness of place, time, quantity, form, causation, and the rest.

This form of lesson is based upon the

observation of child-nature as shown in children's play.

Our own ancestors, never at fault in matters of religion, seem to have understood the revelation made in play, sufficiently to use it for the foundation culture of soul and feeling. The European thinkers and observers,—Pestalozzi, Fröbel, and Cooke—assuming that it is general knowledge of the world that makes man, turned to the same field of study, little children at play, in order to find out from it how the child might be made to acquire this knowledge, and gain a mastery of the world. When we have studied both forms of education, and know all that there is to be known about them, we shall probably be struck by this fact—that the Oriental is always trying to develop the child *within* and the Occidental to put weapons into his hands, by which to subjugate the *without*. It is another instance of the great truth that these civilisations are rather complementary to one another than ultimately antagonistic. And one can only hope that when the problem of general education has been solved for India, there will arise some one to put on eternal record for the world, the science of the Indian *bratas*.

The young of all animals play, and while this may often seem to us aimless and bewildered, we shall generally find on looking closer that the gambols and capers of infancy are at once a dramatisation of the past, and a forecast of the future. The play of kittens is a drama of the hunt. The kid revives the memory of the rocky mountains in which his forbears roamed. This expenditure of energy without immediate return is an overflow of health and strength. The starved have no spirit for play. But while not directly profitable, play is always educational. The cub or the pup is learning his future trade, by those unreasoning movements, repeated over and over again, during the period when he is still dependent for food on his parents. Young birds, by play train themselves for future flying or swimming or scratching of the soil. And the human child, similarly, teaches himself, from the beginning of his life, by spontaneous movements. Mothers know how many are the component efforts by which a baby learns to turn over in bed, to crawl, to walk, to speak. And all these efforts, undertaken wilfully, energetically, repeatedly, are what we regard as play. Yet they are leading, slowly but surely, to the co-ordinated activities of manhood.

When the baby can walk and talk, his mother watches him less closely. Yet the old process is going on, with the same vigour as before, but on an ascending plane of mentality, making, destroying, frolicking alone, playing in groups ; digging, grubbing, modelling clay dolls, investigating mud, sand, water ; catching insects, fish, birds ; throwing balls ; flying kites ; whittling sticks, catching knuckle-bones, imitating weddings and funerals ; taming pigeons ; organising cricket and football ; in all this medley of pursuits, there is no confusion, but a certain definite sequence of progression, corresponding to the mental development of the age. This is nature's way of turning the whole world into the baby's school-room, putting the weapons of his sovereignty into the hands of the future king. Nature makes no mistakes. Under that benign rule, *all* the causes construe to bring into being *all* the effects. And the child's interest never flags. As hunger precedes healthy digestion, so enjoyment accompanies all these lessons. The attention is concentrated, the whole being is absorbed.

The whole of this, however, would in its totality make nothing more than a man of the Stone Age—a great chieftain, loved as leader, mighty in the chase, resourceful, brave, tuneful and a lover of beauty, all this might be produced by Nature's Education, but it is difficult to see very much more. All the rest is the work of man on man, and is initiated in the processes that make up what we call education. Even in the Stone Age these higher elements were at work, or none of us would have emerged from it. Even in the Stone Age, man had his dreams, and woman her hero-tales. Old crones by the hearth-side stood for the children as weird embodiments of wisdom. There was always a super-world for Humanity, of imagination and symbol, of love and hope. As civilisation has grown more complex, this super-world has become more and more definitely an object of aspiration, and enquiry has concerned itself increasingly with the initiation into it of each separate human being. Only with the full elucidation of this question, can there be real hope for man, for only with perfect knowledge of how to educate, can man be rendered independent of birth and inheritance, and stand some chance of being fully humanised. Every religion carries with it its own scheme of initiation, and expresses its own hope and pity for humanity in some form or another. And to-day, having entered upon the age of science,—that age in which secular knowledge constitutes Truth, and is held as sacred as all the scriptures of the past,—it behoves us to formulate, to the best of our ability, that theory of education, by which the human unit is to be *virilised* or initiated into the full powers of Humanity.

'Nature is conquered by obeying her,' says Bacon, and to Pestalozzi,—the great educator who was created by the French Revolution, with its thought of the Rights of Man,—it was clear enough that the science of education could only be built up, on a keen and continuous observation of the laws of mind. Over and over again Pestalozzi refers to the modern problem as that of the "*psychologizing* of education." In this psychologizing, he made two great discoveries. First came the law, that abstract thought has to be gathered from concrete experience. Second was the generalisation, that the child in its development follows the race. One hardly knows which of these two is the more important. In the first place, all knowledge begins with the concrete, that is to say, with the senses. Through the senses to the mind! never by ignoring or thwarting the senses, can we build up education. By *controlling*,—certainly! For control presupposes development, and training is only a larger name for it. But always from experience of the concrete, through the senses, the power of abstract thought, is the great Veda of modern education. It is also the truth that underlies the use of the image in worship, and the *brata* in social culture.

It was on the basis of the law thus enunciated by Pestalozzi, that his disciple, Fröbel, devised the Kinder-garten. For years he watched the play of children, and analysed the subjects they had to learn, trying to connect the one with the other. Finally he invented the collection of toys known as his "gifts"; tabulated a certain number of materials, such as string, sticks, sand, chalk, paper, and others ; and left on record a wonderful series of games and observations. All these things together constitute what is known as the Kindergarten system. It is a system in which all knowledge is supposed to receive a foundation in concrete experience and all work to appear to the child as 'play.' The 'gifts' consist of balls, building-materials, and tiles, for pattern-making. The 'occupations'—such as stick-laying, mat-weaving, paper-folding, colour-drawing, and so on—are of perennial interest, being in fact based on the primitive occupations of humanity. And these games which do not occur simply as parts of lessons, are for the most part observation of the crafts, or of natural phenomena, turned into action-songs. The flight of pigeons, the catching of fish, the sailing of a boat, the work of the peasant, are all subjects that may be described in games, which are often of great spirit.

In every case the educational value of all this depends largely on the particular qualifications of the teacher who is applying it. The Kinder-garten as arranged by Fröbel, is perhaps a thought too complex, a shade too precise, altogether too "German" as one might say. It tends too easily to become mechanical, a hard and fast system, instead of a means to an end. The grasp of fundamental truths and aims, and a certain freedom and generosity in arriving at these, are far more important to the child-gardener than a full supply of material, and a knowledge of Fröbel's sequences. No two Fröbel schools are exactly alike. They will differ, not only in the detail of methods, but also in the dominant conceptions of the function of education. They will differ, also, in the extent to which they avail themselves of the material that has been added—by Cooke and others, from the year 1865 onwards,—to the foundations laid by Fröbel, and the structure erected by him. But if, within the same country and a single village, the difference between various applications of the same principle can be so marked, it follows that the Kinder-garten in Europe and the Kinder-garten in India, ought to be two different things. And no one can create an Indian Kinder-garten, save Indian educators ; for the system must be an efflorescence of Indian life itself, embodying educational principles that are universally true of man. One educator in Bombay, Mr. Chichgar by name, has made attempts during the last fifty years, to Indianise the Kinder-garten, and in certain directions he has succeeded wonderfully. His own face and form are irresistibly suggestive of the typical educator, the creator of educational philosophy. He is curiously like the pictures of Fröbel, in appearance, a mixture of man and mother, both venerable. He has the divine witchery of calling the children to his arms, and he lives for his idea. Undoubtedly Mr. Chichgar has contributed an enormous number of elements of great value to the Indian Kinder-garten of the future. He has concretised the study of number and quantity with great success. But he himself would probably be the first to point out that still further progress in generalising the Kinder-garten is needed, and that the co-operation of every race in India will be necessary before the initiation of learning can be brought to perfection.

The Fröbel school, as we know it, is immensely costly. The idea has suffered from exploitation at the hands of trades-people, till it would seem as if one could not set out to teach a few babies without all sorts of large expenditure. Yet this is directly contrary to the ideal of Fröbel, who must have intended his educational material to be as fugitive and valueless as the broken pots and sticks with which children usually amuse themselves. A very good test for the Indianising of a given toy or occupation would thus lie in finding some object which offered an educational equivalent, without cost. For instance, the first gift Fröbel offers the child* is a soft ball of bright colour. Obviously, for this we must take the common Indian rag ball, and cover it with red, blue, or yellow, green, orange, or purple, cotton. But for a variant on this, we can offer a fruit or a flower, of the requisite tint, dancing on its stem. With these, let the child and its mother, or the children and their teacher, simply play. It is

* Gift I.—Six soft coloured balls, blue, red, yellow, green, orange, and purple in colour.

Gift II.—Ball, cube, and cylinder, in wood, little used in Kindergarten. Chiefly academic.

Gift III.—Cube-like box containing 8 one-inch wooden cubes.

Gift IV.—Box of equal shape and size, containing eight blocks, half the thickness of the former, and twice the length.

true that such balls cannot be made to rebound, but with this exception, they will serve all the purposes of a game, and by their means the child can acquire language, and action collaboration with his fellows. For the rudiments of military precision and uniformity are imparted by means of "ball drilling" or ball-games. The most distinctive feature of the modern school is its class-teaching, as opposed to the individual study, and sing-song in chorus, of mediæval hedge-schools. And class-teaching begins with the united response of several to a signal, as in the case of Fröbel's ball.

Another point to be noted here, is that each perception of the child is to be followed by its appropriate word. First the thing or the act, *then* the name or word. We *feel* the rag-ball with the fingers, and pronounce it *soft*. But every word has its antithesis. 'Show me some thing not soft,' asks the teacher, and the child raps on stone or wood, or what not, pronouncing it hard. Other parallels are found, and 'soft, hard,' is realised and repeated over and over again. After knowing comes language, and each concept has its opposite taught with it. The ball is thrown 'up' then 'down.' The left hand and the right are learnt in one lesson. It is as easy to the child to learn the proper word, in this way, as any simpler substitute for it. We have reached the law : on the subject follows its name, on the deed the word.

Fröbel gives a series of boxes, containing various kinds of bricks for building. These boxes are cubes in shape. The first is divided into eight smaller cubes. The second into eight brick-shaped blocks of equal size and shape ; the third consists of twenty-seven cubes, some of which are divided diagonally into triangular halves and quarters ; and the fourth consists of a cube made of brick-shaped blocks, divided in the same way. These four gifts, and especially the first two of them, are the back-bone of the Kinder-garten. From them the child studies number, geometry, and the dividing of quantities. He listens to a History-story, and makes of them, characters in the tale. They are horses in the hunt ; soldiers in battle ; houses and ghats in geography ; boats, wells, trees, towns, worlds,—everything by turns, and nothing long. Fixed and solid as is their form, they are absolutely fluid to the child's imagination, at once his treasure and his friends. But they are made of wood ; and to describe their form is to imply the skill and precision that went to their making. They cannot but be expensive. For an Indian Kinder-garten, therefore, they are out of the question, unless they could be reproduced in earthen-ware, by the village potter, and so far, I have not once succeeded in having this done, often as I have tried. A substitute for the building gifts is to my own mind, one of the crying needs of the Indian child-garden. In America, however, with this perplexity in mind, I found that theorists did not consider the building-gifts absolutely essential to the Kinder-garten. Prof. John Dewey, indeed,—one of the most distinguished thinkers on these questions—had discarded them altogether, and made large wooden blocks in their place, setting the children free to play with these on the floor, after the common manner of the unschooled child, making trains and engines, and so forth. "The child does not get out of these gifts what we imagine that he gets," was his brief reply, when I asked him his reason for the change. And a great English educator points out that these particular building-gifts are not the *only* way in which the child can be taught to think accurately, to count and divide and arrange. I have wondered, therefore, whether we might not make small *Mâlâs* of dried nuts and seeds,—a ring of eight for the first building-gift, and of twenty-seven for the third—and use these for the number-concepts that could be evolved from the bricks. In such a substitute, we miss, of course, the definition of form, and we miss also the freedom of manipulation, that go with the toys of Fröbel's designing. But unless they can be imitated in half-baked clay, these last cannot be considered available, in India, on any sufficient scale.

II

The whole of a child's time in a Fröbel School is not spent, however, in playing with balls and cubes. There is always the problem of teaching him those things that it is essential to his future he should know, without breaking the spirit of joyousness, or the habit of dealing with the concrete. There is also the question of physical exercise to be provided for. And further there is the need of children and primitive men to *make*, to *create*. The first of these necessities demands that reading, writing, and the like, should be Fröbelised, and included in the school routine. The second is met in a special sense, by games and songs. And the third is the sphere of the *occupations*, in which some material,—like clay, thread, paper, beads, or what not,—is given to the child, and he is taught to make something of it. Only those who have tried, know the marvellous creativeness shown by the children, in modelling, in simple kinds of weaving, in making patterns with coloured chalks, and the like. And on the other hand, few of us have any idea of the intellectual epochs that are made for them by things they have done. The most distinguished man I know tells to this day of a great irrigation work, designed and carried out by him at the age of nine, in a tiny back-garden. The joy with which he succeeded in arranging culverts to carry his canals under the path, is still a stimulus to him, still gives him confidence in himself, in the prime of his life.

These occupations were intended by Fröbel to connect themselves with the primitive occupations of the race. The disciple of Pestalozzi could not forget that each man is to come to maturity by running rapidly through the historic phases of humanity. And it must be this fact that makes the enthusiasm of the child over the occupations so great. When weaving is so simplified that little children can practise it they fall upon it with cries of joy. It is given to them by Fröbel with strips of coloured paper, woven into a paper-frame, or mat, in patterns. It might also be done by weaving coloured string into simple frames of thin bamboo, after the fashion of the toy *chârpois* sold in the bazars. Or strips of coloured rags might be used, instead of string or paper. Or bamboo-shavings might receive different bright colours, and be used for the same purpose.

The delight of the children, and their absorption in this pattern-making, will indicate sufficiently its educational value, for it can not be stated too often, in the words of Herbert Spencer, that appetite is as good a test of mental powers of digestion as of physical.

Mud, clay, and sand are another form of material by whose means children educate themselves. With them, early man learnt to build. Children, and above all Indian children, have a perfect genius for modelling, and this ought to be fostered and encouraged. Let two children make bananas of clay, and by comparing their productions, we shall quickly see which knew more, which observed better, which had proceeded further in thought. From this, we shall quickly learn to see the educational value of modelling, and the intellectual power which expresses itself in all art.

The genius of Fröbel is nowhere seen to greater advantage than when he gives coloured paper to children, and leads them to fold it,—not only, by this means, teaching them an infinitude of geometry, about lines and surfaces, but also encouraging them to make a number of paper-toys. The delight of little children in working together towards a common standard of excellence, makes them pursue eagerly the purposes set before them. And only by trying it, can one begin to understand how much education can be indicated and acquired, by this simple means. The whole mental grasp and development of an individual goes to determine his success in folding a square of paper precisely in half, laying it straight, in its proper place on the table.

It is the scope which they offer to the imagination that makes the little ones love these raw materials of activity, with so ardent a love. None of the costly dolls and other toys that are made by machines and sold in shops, have this power to rouse their interest and absorb their attention. The very crudity of the material is an advantage to the child, because it leaves so much to the mind. It only suggests, it does not complete. Children at play, like the worshipper at prayer, want suggestions of the ideal, not its completed representation. The work of the imagination is something to which we have constantly to invite the child if he does not spring to it spontaneously. It is this which makes him declare, when he receives his first ball, that it is like a bird, a fish, a kitten ; and this first effort of the imagination is to be encouraged, never to be checked.

But an Indian village, far from railways, with its potter, its weaver, its brazier, and its jeweller; with women at the spinning-wheel, and *gowâllâs* tending the animals, is a perfect picture of primitive society. All the early occupations of man are there, and all the early tools. The potter's wheel, the weaver's loom, the plough, the spinning-wheel, and the anvil, are the eternal toys of the race. A child left to play in these streets, dramatising all the life about him, might easily make for himself an ideal Kinder-garten. The village itself is the true child-garden. There is a great deal of truth in this statement. It will always tend to be true in India, that great men for this reason, are born in villages, rather than in cities. And rather in mediæval than in modern cities. At the same time, we must remember that the village is a haphazard congeries of occupations, from the child's point of view, not an organised and directed synthesis, like the school. It is by dramatising the crafts, and repeating them in his own way, that the child educates himself, not by taking an actual part in their labour. If the second of these were the true mode of experience, some slave-child of a servant or a craftsman would stand a better chance of education than the little freeman of a higher class who flits hither and thither at will, and uses labour as a means of self-development, not as a passport to the right of existence.

It is most of all for the stimulus they give to the games, that the child has reason to rejoice in the presence of the village-crafts. A Kindergarten game, ought, ideally, to be a drama constructed impromptu out of a story or a description. It is a drama of the primitive type like that of the *Kathaks* in which one or two principal performers are supported by a chorus. The song is accompanied by such movements as dancing in a ring, hand in hand, clapping, or jumping. The subject may be drawn from nature, or the crafts, or family life. The farmer's labours of sowing, transplanting, and reaping ; the drawing of water for the fields ; the weaver at his loom, and the maiden at her wheel ; the work of potter, brazier and jeweller ; the flight of birds ; the herding of cows ; the life of the river-siders ; the relations of parents and children, all these are good subjects. Mrs. Brander, in Madras, has collected the nursery-rhymes of the Tamils, and made them into simple child-garden games which are of great value in creating enjoyment, and giving co-ordinated action. The children stand in a ring and sing the couplet, with any gestures that may be appropriate. Then, perhaps, they take hands and dance round, repeating it. Such games, of pure physical movement, deserve inclusion in the Kinder-garten list. The well-known rhyme in Bengali, beginning, *"Tâi, Tâi, Tâi, Mâmâr bâdi jái,"* suggests similar treatment.

The most serious and universally applicable aspects of the Kinder-garten are discovered, however, so soon as we begin to consider the problem of initiating, through them, various kinds of knowledge. Without breaking the continuity of its concrete experience, the child has to learn the use of written language, Arithmetic, Geometry, History, Geography, various kinds of science and design. In leading its mind into the struggle with these different classes of facts, we are free to use any object or material that pleases us, or promises to illustrate the task before us. But certain principles must guide us. We must present the child with appropriate elements, that is to say, with elements that he can deal with. And we must lead him to learn, through his own deeds. I have often thought that a box full of little card-board tiles, printed with the letters of the alphabet, would be a more child-like way of teaching a child to read, than a reading book. The learning would be more rapid and more pleasant, if these letters were to be picked out and put together, like the pieces of a puzzle. Certainly writing comes before reading, just as speaking a foreign language precedes the easy understanding of it. Word-building,—the spelling of detached words—comes before the reading of sentences. And so on. Always the appeal to the senses. Always the learning by experience. And always joy, the hunger for more.

Many people fear if work be always made delightful, children will be enervated, and become unable to do that which is distasteful and hard. But these minds have missed the whole meaning of the child-garden. The joy that the child feels there, is the joy of self-control, the joy of energy and absorption, the joy of work. It is an austere, not a libertine, delight. A well-trained Kinder-garten child knows better than any other how to address himself to a new problem, how to shoulder a heavy load, how to infer a principle, from the facts to be correlated. And this power has been gained by teaching him in accordance with his own nature, by watching the laws of his development, and seeking to run with these, instead of against them, by enlisting the activity and effort of the whole child, instead of fettering some faculties and dictating to others.

In other words, if the aim of the Kindergarten has been realised at all, Nature has here been conquered by obeying her.

MANUAL TRAINING AS A PART OF GENERAL EDUCATION IN INDIA.

If we are to make anything like a complete outline of the study known as Manual Training, for the use of Indian Schools and teachers, it will first be necessary to define very clearly the four stages into which a typical educational course may be divided.

For the purposes of this paper, then, we shall consider *Primary*, or Vernacular, or Village Education, as an essential part of a thorough education, and as lasting up to the age of eight, or at most ten years in the case of an Indian boy of the higher classes. During this period, the only language dealt with is the vernacular ; method of learning is of infinitely greater importance than information imparted. The child ought to learn to think, and discover, and also to create for himself ; spontaneous activity of mind and body has a value far beyond that of discipline ; and if any single formal system of teaching is to be taken as type and centre, it must certainly be the Kinder-garten. *Secondary Education*, next, may be considered as covering in a boy's life, the years that lie between eight and twelve, or ten and fourteen, or there-abouts. During these years, the child probably begins the study of English, and recapitulates in that language the little that he may previously have acquired, of formal instruction in his own. It is to be hoped, however, for the sake of intellectual integrity and clearness, that the bulk of his education continues to be given in the vernacular, which alone, a boy of this age can possibly be capable of understanding thoroughly.

At twelve or fourteen, as the case may be, the lad will enter on what we may call his *High School Course*. This, in India to-day, is probably carried on almost entirely in English ; and while we may deplore this fact, we may possibly have to admit its necessity. For no Indian vernacular can give any one freedom of communication throughout the whole country, and while Hindustani, or Urdu goes near to satisfying this test, English is still the more advantageous, in as much as it confers the lingual franchise, not of India alone, but of the world as a whole, and is, further, a *modern* language, by whose means can be obtained an exactness of thought which is the key to many languages and to almost all the culture, of the present age. In the High School stage of education, there is definite preparation for the work of colleges and universities, which is to come after. And the life's task is probably selected during these years. Nevertheless, our boy is not yet a man. He is still learning. His mistakes are not yet crimes. And the demands of a growing body for plenty of wholesome food and vigorous exercise, for light and air and abundance of pure water, ought to take precedence still of all other necessities, though it ought never to be dissociated from the still keener and manlier joys of increasing self-mastery and intellectual conquest.

And last of all comes the *College Career,* which begins at sixteen or eighteen, and ends at twenty or twenty-two years of age, as the case may be. It is perhaps worth while to say here that in matters educational there is no substitute for time. It is a mistake to imagine that an education finished at twenty represents the enjoyment of an advantage over that which is finished at twenty-two. In ninety-nine cases out of a hundred, the reverse is the case. Culture is at bottom a question of *growth,* of development, both of brain and body ; and just as we cannot 'rush' a human being through an appointed cycle of physiological changes in a period of time arbitrarily determined, so we cannot act in the corresponding fashion intellectually. The best educated Indian man whom I have seen, left the village school at nine, and ended a second university career in England at twenty-six years of age. The more generous we can be about time, the better results we shall be able to show educationally, and the better worth while it becomes, to consider the question of educational methods.

At any rate, the recognition of Manual Training as a part of General Education leads to no cheapening or curtailing of the scheme as a whole. It is always, expensive, more or less, in any particular case, according to the form which is given to it and the completeness with which it is practised. And it always adds to the time required for education. In a Manual Training High School, in the United States, half of the total school time, that is to say, from twelve to fifteen hours a week, is given to drawing and other manual training occupations. Of these twelve to fifteen hours not more than five are assigned to drawing of various kinds, in some cases including clay-modelling and wood-carving,—an equal time is given to wood work, as practised in carpentry and by the joiner—and another equal number of hours is devoted to metal work, that is, Vice-work, black-smithing, tin-smithing, and machine construction. At the Manual Training High School which is connected with the University at St. Louis, the combined courses in wood and metal are never allowed to take more than eight hours a week ; but in this case, freehand, mechanical, and architectural drawing are treated altogether as a separate subject, occupying another four or five hours.

Now it is not to be understood that these courses are added to the ordinary curriculum of arts with a view to fitting school-boys for manufacturing or business careers. Undoubtedly, if a boy on leaving school wishes to devote himself to commercial work of any kind, his initiation into it is made easy, by the fact that he is already accustomed to bringing his mind to bear on kindred problems, and calling up all his intellectual resources to aid in their solution. Undoubtedly this is the case. But the argument for the necessity of Manual Training does not rest on such observations as this. It rests entirely on the nature of the human nervous system, and on known facts regarding the correlation of brain-centres with the development of physical impression and expression. It is entirely from this point of view that we have a right to plead for its inclusion in the school-course. If it were only calculated to supply the factory and the warehouse with competent organisers and directors, the community might well insist on leaving to the mercantile classes, the responsibility of creating opportunities for a limited amount of such training. But those whose experience gives them a right to speak, will in every case maintain that, other things being equal, a boy who was had manual training is in all ways the intellectual superior of him who has not. He has freshness and vigour of thought, due to the fact that he knows how to observe, and is accustomed to think for himself. He has daring and originality of purpose. And above all, his character is based on the fundamental habit of adding deed to dream, act to thought, proof to inference.

Over and over again in University register or syllabus do American educators insist upon this,—the purely *educational* purpose of manual training. Say the experts of St. Louis—"If the object is Education, the skilful teacher has no function except to teach......In a manual training school, *everything is for the benefit of the boy ; he is the most important thing in the shop ; he is the only article to be put upon the market.* Even in manual education the chief object is mental development and culture. Manual derterity is but the evidence of a certain kind of mental power, and this mental power, coupled with a knowledge of materials and a familiarity with the tools the hand uses, is doubtless the only basis of that sound practical judgment and ready mastery of material forces and problems which always characterises one well-fitted for the duties of active life. Hence the primary object is the acquirement of mental clearness and intellectual acumen." Even a lawyer should be a better lawyer, if he have had manual training.

The University of St. Louis goes on to point out that, ideally, manual training ought to have a general, rather than a specific character, if its possible economic application is to have the widest range. "We therefore abstract all the mechanical processes, and manual arts, and typical tools, of the trades and occupations of men, and arrange a systematic course of instruction in the same. Thus, without teaching any trade, we teach the essential mechanical principles which underlie all mechanical trades." A very significant insight into the nature of the work done in the school room, is here afforded. There is a marked difference between the practice of a trade as such, and its use for educational purposes. If the two were the same, the object of manual training might be served by putting a boy into an artisan's workshop for a certain number of hours every week. But they are not the same. To learn to make furniture is not the same thing, by any means, as to acquire accuracy, facility, and executive ability, by working at the cutting and fitting of wood. To learn to make watches or clocks is not the same thing as to be disciplined and experienced in the use of wheels, springs, and pendulums, and to understand theoretically,—so that the mind can use the knowledge,—the physical resistance of one material or another. The educational value of modern industries can only be gathered from a generalisation of those industries, re-analysed into its educative elements. Such a generalisation has been made in America, with the result that a Manual Training High School arranges its course of work, according to the plan given in a table in the appendix, at the end.

That table has been in the main, extracted from an interview with Dr. Hanford Henderson on Technical Education in America and Japan, which was published in the *Hindu* of Madras, in April 1904. But reference to the Special

Bulletin, (Whole Number 286) which has been published by the Bureau of Education, Washington, D. C., giving synopses of the courses of study in eighteen Manual Training High Schools, confirms Dr. Hanford Henderson's in every particular as an accurate and representative abstract of what is necessarily the time-table of all manual training courses at this stage of a boy's education.

From this American state paper, can also be gathered the details of an ideal course of Manual Training, extending over three or four years, for girls, of between twelve and twenty years of age.

In this case, the outlook of the work done, is upon art and home-life. The usual drawing, and some work in water-colours, cooking and domestic science (house-work), sewing, clay-modelling, and wood-carving, make up the first year's curriculum. In the second year we have drawing again, dress-making, clay-modelling, wood-carving, and work in ornamental cut iron. As an art, the last mentioned subject is spurious, consisting, as it does, of making pretty trifles out of curved bits of ribbon-iron, fastened together neatly by the pliers. But as an opportunity for learning design and mastering the use of certain important tools, it deserves considera tion. In this second year, the practical teaching of cooking, is superseded by theoretical lessons on the chemistry of food and its preparation.

The third and fourth years simply carry these and similar courses into more advanced developments, and nursing of children and of the sick, first aid to the injured, and laundry-work find a place amongst the subjects which receive theoretical and practical recognition.

Two other parts of the education there are, further, which cannot be ignored by those who would frame manual training courses, whether for boys or girls. These are science and gymnastics. To attempt to give manual training, without some theoretic knowledge, however elementary, of Mechanics, Physics, and Chemistry, and without the deliberate culture of the powers of observation with regard to plants, animals, and the outside world generally, is like trying to divorce the hand from the eye, or both from the mind. And in the same way, the efficient schoolmaster cannot fail to recognise that his pupils have bodies, which ought, *as bodies,* to be recognised and developed. Football and cricket are doing a fine work outside the school-house, but they are apt to serve the successful best. We want something which fulfils the test of a good lesson, by causing proportionate self-development of the highest and lowest talent at the same moment. In most English schools of the kind we are considering, this want is met by giving an hour or two in the week to military drill. And this we do, as well for girls as for boys. I could wish that the custom obtained in Indian schools! The instructor is usually some retired soldier, who, as "drill-sergeant," is glad to add something to his modest resources, and is often very popular with his pupils. When we consider on the one hand, how much the Indian people need to be disciplined in habits of co-operation, and in the mind and feeling of united action, and when we realise, on the other, the immense subconscious influence of orderly marching, wheeling, charging, forming squares, covering, doubling, obeying words of command with regard to imaginary weapons, and the rest, we cannot but believe that a great part of the Indian problem is capable of an educational solution, by this very simple means, in the school compound!

The next question which will occur to a practical Indian mind, with regard to the institution of manual training as a feature of general education, is its cost. I must confess that when I saw the manual training departments of some of the American High Schools, I was overwhelmed, at once with admiration and dismay, —admiration at the generosity with which the American people provide for their own educational needs, and dismay when I contemplated the possibility of Indian competition. The High School of the Pratt Institute in Brooklyn, contains, for instance, complete equipments of carpenters' benches, vices and tools; forges, furnaces, engines, and metal-casting apparatus. And all this entirely apart from the strictly Technical Department for which the Institute is famous. Here, during a time equivalent to a third of the school-week, everybody will be found, in his turn, with the appearance of a strong and intelligent workman, gaining practical experience of such machinery as in India is only to be seen in a few ship-yards, mines, and factories. Can there be any doubt as to the advantage derived from such opportunities, or the desirability of creating the like here?

At the same time, if we only remember that the main purpose of manual training is, after all, *educational* rather than industrial, we shall see that, as we say in Europe, half a loaf is better than no bread. In other words, it is best to begin where we can. A union of two or three far-sighted Indian merchants, anxious for the future of industry in this country, would be sufficient to establish manual training high schools, and technical schools of the College Grade, in the capital of the different presidencies. And Indian Sovereigns might do likewise, each in his own State. But the impossibility of furnishing their schools with princely completeness, ought not to deter the rank and file of head-masters from considering simple means of giving useful manual training to their boys.

According to figures furnished by Dr. Henderson, a good manual training equipment for wood and metal work *without* machine construction, means a capital outlay of about 165 rupees per boy—*i.e.* Wood-work 75 rupees, Vice-work (metal) 30 rupees, Blacksmithing 60 rupees. For little more than 3,000 rupees, therefore, a school could be fitted for twenty pupils, in everything except machine construction, and as this twenty need take only five hours at most in any one course, the outfit would really represent sufficient for a school of one hundred and twenty boys,—or even more, if Saturdays, Sundays, and evenings, could be utilised for classes. It must be admitted that machine construction would be a serious blank in the programme ; and yet, the advantage of having such an institution though suffering from this want, in every city, can hardly be realised. In the estimate given, moreover, we are considering only cost of outfit, and not that of maintaining the school, which would depend on the salaries paid to teachers, rent, and other items varying locally.

It will have been inferred by this time, that the high school stage of education is the heart of the manual training idea, considered as an element in general culture. The studies which it covers, if carried to the college, or university grade, must be pursued with the definite purpose of preparation for future work. As such, they become normal courses—that is, a division of educational science,—or else take their place in the curriculum of civil or mining engineering which may be laid down by the particular university in question.

As a matter of fact, however, a boy who can afford during these years to qualify himself for a distinct industrial profession will be likely to choose, not a university, but a *Technical School* course.

It has been said that a man who is to take a high position in the world of industry ought to pass from the manual training school to the university, and after completing his general education there, return to the technical institute, and spend two years in special technical preparation. Such a piece of advice enables us to estimate the culture-rank of technical schools in the American sense. They are not simply schools for artisans. They are too costly. They are, in their highest classes, colleges for the chiefs and captains of industry. They are in fact to Labour, what the University is to intellectual culture.

With regard to the history of that idea which is embodied in the technical schools of America, and the polytechnics of the continent of Europe, we may take our facts from the report of an English royal commission published in the year 1882.

The beginnings of the modern industrial system had been due, in the main, to Great Britain. Factories founded on the inventions of Watt, Arkwright, and Crompton, were for many years, an English monopoly, and when about the year 1840, other European countries began to construct railways and to erect modern mills, and mechanical workshops, they found themselves face to face with a full-grown industrial organisation in Great Britain, which was almost a sealed book to those who could not obtain access to her factories.

"To meet this state of things abroad, foreign countries established technical schools like the Ecole Centrale of Paris, and the polytechnic schools of Germany and Switzerland, and sent engineers and men of science to England, to prepare themselves for becoming teachers of technology in those schools.

"Technical high schools now exist in nearly every Continental State, and are the recognised channel for the instruction of those who are intended to become the technical directors of industrial establishments. Many of the technical chemists have, however been, and are being, trained in the German Universities. Your commissioners believe that the success which has attended the foundation of extensive manufacturing establishments, engineering shops, and other works on the Continent, could not have been achieved to its full extent in the face of many retarding influences, had it not been for the system of high technical instruction in these schools, for the facilities for carrying on original scientific investigation, and for the general appreciation of the value of that instruction and of original research which is felt in those countries.

.... "The buildings are palatial, the laboratories and museums are costly and extensive, the staff of professors.........is so numerous as to admit of the utmost sub-division of the subjects taught. In Germany, the attendance at some of the polytechnic schools has lately fallen off, chiefly because the supply of technically trained persons is in excess of the present demand ; certainly not because it is held that the training of the school can be dispensed with."

These English commissioners speak strongly of the general culture and liberal education which is required of the masters and managers of great factories and other industrial establishments on the continent of Europe. They speak of the knowledge which these men possesses of the sciences upon which their particular industry depends ; of their familiarity with new scientific discoveries ; of their promptitude in adopting all the improvements, made either in their own country, or in the world at large, thanks to their knowledge of foreign languages, and of conditions of manufacture prevalent outside. In all this, we see that the strength of continental training may be taken as lying in its strong background of disinterested, scientific knowledge, and England's industrial distinction again, as dependent on her great workshops, which the same commissioners declare to be "the best technical schools in the world." The American annotation upon the English report, made in the year 1885, adds that in RUSSIA the technical education ideas of the rest of Europe have been "expanded into schools which surpass in completeness of equipment and affluence of resources, any in the other countries of Europe, with the possible exception of the Ecole Polytechnique at Paris." And to this it may be added that on the *Mechanical* side of technical instruction, probably no other country can approach the great network of technical institutions spread over the United States to-day.

In these schools, a four years' course is offered in :—

(*a*) Mechanical Engineering, that is, Machine construction ;

(*b*) Electrical Engineering, the making of Electrical Machinery ;

(*c*) Civil Engineering ;

(*d*) Architecture ; and

(*e*) The Physical and Chemical processes, constituting various industries and manufactures.

Thus, it is clear that the technical school is simply an Engineering College, and as we should expect, the student has to pass, at entrance, certain mathematical and general literary tests.

The best college of this class in America is said to be the Massachusetts Institute of Technology at Boston. But the enormous wealth of the Leland-Stanford University of California makes it probable that its Engineering department will quickly form a technical college of at least equal rank.

Before leaving this aspect of the subject, and directing our attention entirely to those forms of manual training which might be applied to the present moment to Indian educational requirements, there is one more point to be dealt with, and that is the provision made in America for turning out *teachers* for manual training high schools, and the question of how to use that provision for the organisation of such facilities in India.

With regard to the United States, Dr. Hanford Henderson unhesitatingly describes, as the ideal curriculum, a year spent at the Sloyd Training School in Boston, and then a second year at the Teachers' College, Columbia University, New York. After this, a tour of the schools themselves,—of which the best are said to be in Chicago and Philadelphia,—would be an absolute necessity. And then, provided the men who receive the training be "thorough, not afraid of hard work, strong and alert in body, quick and broad in mind, and sympathetic and sincere in heart, the cause of manual training in India should be in secure hands."

Even in America, a good deal of anxiety has been experienced by educators, as to the form which preparatory courses in manual training ought to take, during what we have here designated as the secondary stage in a complete education, that is to say, the years between eight and twelve.

To meet this need, simple courses have been arranged under such names as "card-board modelling," and "Sloyd," in which, with the aid of a few simple tools, boys and girls can learn to make easy objects in card-board or in wood.

To take card-board modelling first: Let a child be provided with a piece of strawboard, or white cardboard printed in ¼ inch chequers; a stout penknife, pencil, measuring ruler, compasses, and india-rubber. Let the teacher, then standing at the blackboard, *dictate*, and draw in chalk on the board, with larger instruments, the lines and measurements necessary, in order to make, say, a square-folded envelope. This done, let him next explain along what lines the knife must be drawn sharply, to make an incision, and along which gently, that the card may afterwards be folded. This is done, and a square envelope has been modelled in cardboard.

The next lesson will perhaps treat similarly the construction of a box, and the lid for the box ; a photograph-frame ; a purse ; a book-cover or folded portfolio ; or what not. Solid forms of polygonal outline are treated next, the time soon comes when the children hasten to be beforehand with the teacher in suggesting new problems and working out the method of attack. And when this happens we know that education is actually being achieved, for, what is this but the simultaneous bestowal in each study of a new step to be ascended, and the will to mount?

Sloyd or school wood-work, is not so easy a matter to treat. It is necessary to have a special room equipped with suitable benches and tools. It is suggested that if the individual sloyd-bench be found too expensive, a strong table with vices attached, accommodating four pupils, may be used. Appropriate wood and the usual drawing instruments have next to be supplied, and these include pencils, rulers, and compasses. Amongst tools enumerated for this simplified woodwork, I find the plane, splitting saw, bit-brace, drill-bit, back saw, hammer, screw-driver, centre-bit, half-round file, turning saw, spoke-shave, cross-cut saw, knife, compass saw, sand-paper, and others. Sets of the necessary instruments including the table are estimated by the Sloyd Training School, Boston, Massachusetts, as costing something over one hundred rupees for four pupils.

Having made this expenditure, the teacher proceeds to utilise it by producing such articles as photograph shelves, almanac stands, the seat for a swing, handkerchief boxes, glove boxes, small model carts, and so on. This work is supposed to provide for vigorous muscular activity, and to stimulate spontaneous creativeness.

Most of us will think, however, that such a statement stands self-condemned. It seems as if the adoration of mechanical ability were running away with the American educator. All this trouble and outlay, merely for the sake of antedating the manual school's benchwork by a few years! It would appear, too, that for the sake of learning the use of the latest thing in tools, the necessity for skill of hand tends to be minimised, and manual training courses, carried to a foolish extravagance by a wealthy people, may end by defeating the very object for which they were instituted. If India is to have manual training in her schools, it must be, obviously, by less elaborate means than these, and vigorous muscular activity will have to be sought in other ways than through "Elementary Sloyd," as organised in the given case.

The wise man, however, knows how to take a hint, even when he refuses complete direction, and simple educational courses might probably be devised, in which accurate measurement and constructive ability should be evolved gradually, in true relation at once to theoretic knowledge and concrete application in wood.

Boys of from eight to twelve, provided with hammer, knife, saw, and screw-driver, or with a single tool-box for a small class, might make many articles of household and personal use, with immense advantage to themselves.

All good teachers know how to test the value of their own instruction by the interest which they can rouse in their pupils. Even if we have not read Herbert Spencer s little book on "Education," we have probably considered and appreciated its main argument, namely that, as a healthy physical appetite seeks valuable food-elements spontaneously, and rejects those which are injurious, so a child who is being well-trained, loves those studies that he needs, and hates those only which are bad, or are badly presented to him. In other words, the teacher who can maintain the interest of the boys is a good teacher. The lesson that delights a class is a good lesson. So the method of teaching even simple carpentry may differ in different cases, but the test remains,—if taught so that the pupils love the work, it is well-taught.

Thus we have considered the American system of Manual Training as a feature of general education. Says Professor William James of Harvard, in words which sum up the whole claims :—

"The most colossal improvement which recent years have seen in secondary education lies in the introduction of the manual training schools; not because they will give us a people more handy and practical for domestic life and better skilled in trades, but because they will give us citizens with an entirely different intellectual fibre. Laboratory work and shop work engender a habit of observation, a knowledge of the difference between accuracy and vagueness, and an insight into nature's complexity and into the inadequacy of all verbal accounts of real phenomena, which once wrought into the mind, remain there as lifelong possessions. They confer precision...........They give honesty...........They beget a habit of self-reliance...........They occupy the pupil in a way most congruous with the spontaneous interests of his age. They absorb him, and leave impressions durable and profound. Compared with the youth taught by these methods, one brought up exclusively on books carries through life a certain remoteness from reality; he stands, as it were, out of the pale, and feels that he stands so; and often suffers a kind of melancholy from which he might have been rescued by a more real education."

"Citizens with an entirely different intellectual fibre,"—to produce these is undoubtedly the main purpose of all genuine manual training. It is a right and reasonable purpose, to which the means taken are well adapted.

But as we look at the actual scheme for the achievement of the end, adopted by American thinkers and teachers, we have to admit that there is also another and subsidiary purpose, of which the educational organiser is less conscious, probably, whose existence even he might perhaps be unwilling to acknowledge. But it is there. And this is a desire to recognise and during school-years to recapitulate effectively within the school-walls, the main features of the great mechanical and industrial civilisation without.

Why should the high school stage of education include a course of study of all the modern industries *in extenso*, with their appropriate tools, and end in a year's work at machine construction, in which, as we are told, "we have the assembling together of all the other branches"? What does this mean, if not that the transition from tool to machine,—which has been made more or less anarchically by the societies of the West,—is to be bridged over, intellectually and morally, for the fully equipped individual of the future?

The necessity for manual training of some kind is rightly felt in America to be a fact inherent in human psychology generally, and in the psychology of education, in particular. But the *form* which manual training takes in that country is quite equally the result of the typical civilisation of the day. A well-educated man must have been trained in the use of his hands. True, and a well-educated man of the modern world, must also, in the course of this training, have learnt the fundamental principles of machinery, and its use. He must know the essential facts about the making of steam-engines to work the school pumps, dynamos, electric motors, and all the smaller machinery that can be built in any well-equipped commercial worship. Not only the transition from tool to machine, but also that from steam to electricity, then, is foreseen and provided for intellectually before the boy is released from tutelage, to find or to win his own place on the world's battle-field. The wisdom and foresight of this principle cannot be disputed, and its application to Indian education is still more obvious. If America, with her workshops and dock-yards, her manufacture of machinery and her scientific laboratories, cannot afford to ignore the Mechanic Age in her school-rooms, how much less can India, for whom the immediate (though not final) problem is of her own entrance into that age? We can imagine indeed, that a wise statesman of Indian blood might say to himself, "Let me only create during school-years, enough men who understand and can construct modern mechanism, and the future of the country may take care of itself." For it is undoubted that if the Indian nation possessed the necessary knowledge, the advent of the Mechanic Age could not be long delayed.

When we come to the study of the pre-modern phase of industry, however, we begin to understand what is the weak point in the American development. It is quite clear that those industries and implements which preceded the modern mechanical consolidation historically, should also precede it educationally. In the Secondary Education stage, then, every Indian village can furnish the elements of a better course in manual training than could be commanded in any American city. Such old-world material as the brick-kiln and the potter's wheel, the spinning-wheel and simple hand-loom, the distaff and spindle for preparing wool, the dyeing vat, and the old recipes for vegetable colours, the brazier's fire and tools, the glass-blower's furnace, or even the split cane and dried palm-leaves of the basket-weaver's use, all these are capable of being turned to account educationally, by one who unites the knowledge of their use to a wide intellectual training, and a thorough familiarity with educational principles.

The student of history knows how in Ancient Greece the making and decoration of simple pottery of the Asiatic domestic order, grew into one of the most memorable of the world's arts. He knows, too, that China, carriyng out a similar development of the "vase," along a different line, and arriving early at the invention of porcelain, has enjoyed a ceramic evolution entirely distinct and yet as nobly characteristic as the Hellenic. Nor does he forget the wonderful colouring and design of Delhi, Lahore, and Persia, in his study of baked clays.

Such knowledge on the part of the teacher makes it possible to introduce clay, wheel, and firing-oven into the school-house as essential parts of a liberal, and not of an artisan's education.

The history of the great Indian art of cotton-printing, again, finds illustration in every village, and would give stimulus and encouragement to any child, in learning that use of the hands which constitutes manual training. Or the plaiting of dyed grasses, palm-leaves, and split bamboo might be made at once an occasion for carrying on a simple order of weaving, and for giving an outlook into the history of materials, articles of use, and even textile fabrics.

At first, and perhaps always, the only way to teach such arts would be by bringing the craftsman to ply his trade in the midst of the class, in the presence of a fine teacher who would know how to question, guide, and comment on the work done. And in such communion between humble worker and educated boys, qualifying themselves to become some day the leaders of their people, lies a union of worlds which is worth striving for.

The old carpenter, or weaver, or potter, or what not, is something of *guru* and something of ministrant in one, and through him his pupils may come into loving touch with a world which otherwise is likely to pass away, unrecorded, misunderstood, mourned too late.

We are supposing that the manual training of this secondary stage of education is to be given an industrial bent. It might equally well be made artistic. In that case modelling and design would be the principal subjects taught. The materials—rice-flour, vermillion, white and yellow earths—are found in every village and in every household. The subjects might vary from *âlpanâ*-patterns and *sâdi*-borders, to cotton printing, incised tiles and dishes of black earthen-ware, and the wonderful modellings for door-ways and house-fronts, which are common in Benares and other old cities.

Decorative ability is as common in India as earth and water. Every humble builder has ideas and feelings about architectural loveliness. Every woman can make beautiful patterns. Every child has an instinctive love for soft and delicate colour. And the innate power of modelling—of giving solid and plastic form to ideas of beauty—is incredible. But we have as yet no one who understands the value and relation of all these, so as to be able to call them into consciousness and self-direction. Such work might be initiated in the secondary school.

The object of manual training in this country will not be the *acquisition* of manual dexterity: this already exists, thanks largely, no doubt, to the habit of eating with the fingers. The object of the training, in India, must lie in the *intellectualising* of the existing faculty; in the power given to estimate rightly and to direct wisely the ability we already have; in the opportunity which can only come through concrete labour and experience to understand and contrast duly, the old civilisation and the new. If a boy could go through a whole course of this training, graduated, as has been suggested, from the first moment of education, in his fifth or sixth year, to the very end, in an Engineering University, elaborately fitted up, I do not hesitate to say that he would understand the past and the future of India, and be in a position to become a statesman, and a leader of society, different in maturity and balance of knowledge, from any that we have yet seen.

That education of the subconscious intellect which it is claimed that manual training only can effect, might well stand or fall by such a test. And the worlds of refreshment and delight which are hidden in it at all stages for the literary student, though not a main argument for the benefits which it confers, are upspringing witnesses at each step, to tell us that we are on the true path.

It is not necessary to do more than touch on the Primary, or Kinder-garten, stage of education. It was the great educator, Pestalozzi,—the Ŝaint of the sense of Humanity,—who discovered that only by modern "Anschauung,"—looking-at, or as he defined it, "sense impression, thought germination, expression," —and not by words, could knowledge be built up. Fröbel, the father of the Kinder-garten, was Pestalozzi's disciple, applying the *guru's* great principle to the early stages of a child's development. The Kinder-garten therefore is neither more nor less than an attempt to begin every kind of learning with concrete experience, and the handling of wood, clay, wool, rags, paper, running water, pencil, colour, and other materials, in organised and purposeful ways, forms its most distinctive educational element. All this, without tools, leads up to the simple old tools of the race—wheel, loom, kiln,—in the secondary stage, as we have been considering it. On this, again, should be superposed the American development of mechanical-manual training. And if the organising of education in this fashion could only succeed in attracting some of our finest Indian intellects, I should not hesitate to prophesy that fifteen years hence the West would be seeking from India the means of giving manual training in the secondary stage of education, as India is now seeking from the West, the knowledge of how to give it in high school and college.

MANUAL TRAINING IN EDUCATION—SUPPLEMENTARY NOTE.

The visit of Dr. Hanford-Henderson—the great United States specialist on manual training,—has made such an impression throughout the country on those who are wisely interested in the bettering of educational methods, that it is necessary to add from time to time to the information which he scattered broadcast while here.

Dr. Hanford-Henderson, as will be remembered, made a strong distinction between (*a*) industrial or trade-schools ; (*b*) manual training as a factor in general education ; and (c) technical education ; all three alike, as it should scarcely be necessary to point out, lying outside the range of distinctively scientific work. Of these, there can be no doubt that the most important, in the larger sense, is the second, namely manual training as a factor in general education. Regarding this, Dr. Henderson said :

"It soon became apparent that, as a scheme of intellectual development, it was too important to be omitted from the education even of those boys who were intended for the learned professions. From having a merely industrial outlook, manual training came to have a much broader educational purpose. It is now given all over America in the course of secondary education, not only in the High Schools but also increasingly in the lower schools, as a means of culture quite as much, or even more than, as a means to direct bread and butter making. *We invariably find that a manual training boy can do better work in mathematics and in other studies requiring original thought than one who has not this training*."

But while manual training in schools is in this way so vastly more important than the question either of industrial or technical schools, it is at the same time hampered by the fact that it is not, like them, a means to direct money-earning. In our Western industrial and trade schools, a girl or boy learns cooking, sewing, carpentering, shoe-making or what not, with the simple view of at once going out into the world and finding a place in that particular trade. Up to the present, in India, the caste-system has obviated the necessity of such schools by making a man s trade hereditary and the home of the craftsman an industrial school. The son of the jeweller or the *dhobie* learns his life-task from babyhood, as we know ; and if new needs, which can not be wholly supplied in this way, are making themselves felt to-day, still, the English work-shop or factory is at present doing the work of educating to some extent in the particular task required those whom it employs. And India has not as yet understood the necessity of organising craft-knowledge in that relation to modern science which we may regard as true industrial education. She will probably realise this necessity first in the direction of agriculture and some of the allied pursuits, such as silk-culture, market-gardening and so on.

Technical education is something whose need the higher castes in India are in a position at once to understand, and of which they have made every effort,—short of themselves creating adequate opportunities,—to avail themselves. Technical education has the advantage of offering a handsome livelihood to the man who has been so fortunate as to secure it. It is indeed astonishing that many of the Native States should not long ago have seen the inevitableness of having sooner or later to develope and organise themselves in a modern sense and sent out large numbers of young men to the technical schools of America, Japan and

Europe, in order that when that time should come they might be in a position to give the work to their own subjects instead of to Europeans. There are so many tasks still undone in India, tasks which the Native States might easily take up on their own initiative, tasks of sanitation, of replanting of forests, of road and bridge-making, of canal-cutting and cleaning, of railway-making, and what not, that there is still plenty of room for reform in this matter, plenty of time for Indian princes and men of wealth to show themselves statesmen, by taking the wise and far-sighted course.

Still, technical and industrial education could at any time be added to the national resources in the course of a single generation, on the sole condition of the existence of a guiding mind with a great enough ambition and command of sufficient revenues. Manual Training, as a factor in literary education is in a different position. It leads to no direct making of money, in the case of the boy trained. A Brahmin will not turn carpenter merely because he has had lessons in woodwork included in his school course. He will certainly, however, prove himself more manly and original in all that he undertakes, whether of thought or character. The indirect influence of manual training, that is to say, its educational value, is beyond prize. But its direct uses are not so obvious. And in proportion to its greater value is also the greater difficulty of incorporating it in the general educational scheme of an entire State. This is not merely a question of money and 'plant'. It is far more a matter of the degree to which the educational idea itself has been assimilated and a particular form of work made the means of its expression. And this is in its turn a question of time as well as personalities. Hence manual training in its first inception must take the form of an experiment at headquarters, as it were, and under the most favourable circumstances it requires a considerable period to become systematised and established. Manual training, again, is not cheap. On the other hand, as Dr. Henderson has pointed out, "the return is so valuable, both socially and economically, that the expenditure is justified a hundred-fold. A fully-supplied Manual Training School costs more for equipment than an equally fine classical school, but it need not cost much more to operate. It is in this case, as in so many others, the first step that costs."

The desiderata then being so great, it is a delightful surprise to find that the point on which Dr. Henderson has best succeeded in rousing Indian curiosity and interest is precisely this of manual training schools. And the question that naturally comes first is, "How can manual training be introduced into schools for the first time?"

In answer to this question, we have to remember that in the West, manual training is more in harmony with the exigencies of life and institutions than in the East. That is to say, custom itself creates a certain preparedness in the pupil. The great luxury of common life in England and America demands the power of mastering practical detail in every individual more or less. And this demand is aided and abetted by the strictness of the standard of public order.

Then, again, in the ideal education, the Kinder-garten precedes and the play-ground accompanies the manual training stage of education. Cricket and tennis are no mean collaborators of the effort to attain manual skill, and, in England at least, the boy or girl who grew pale over books without attempting to take exercise, would be despised amongst school-fellows as lazy, or worse. Hard physical labour by way of pleasure, is perhaps the *tapas* of the West, corresponding to the prayers and fasting of the East. And I cannot forget how on the last Charrok Puja day of the Swami Vivekananda's life, he announced to me, *à propos* of some games at Belur, that in future the Hindu's Charrok Puja ought to be spent in a gymnasium!

Let us then suppose a well-equipped Western school, duly provided with Kindergarten, play-grounds and fine teachers, what would be the manual training history of a boy passing through it? This is a practical question and will serve perhaps to display the character of a Western training better than any other method.

From the moment of entering the Kindergarten, the child is learning that co-ordination of faculty through hand, eye, and mind, that is afterwards to be carried so much further in the higher schools. The materials used are simple and consist of such things as the little one would have been likely to seize on, in his own play,—mud, sand, paper, wool and small objects, hard and soft. But what seems so meaningless to us is a *sâdhana* to the childish mind. Every faculty is intensely concentrated while the fingers are trying to fashion a mud pot, or cut a paper flower; and if any one doubts that the pre-occupation is worth while.

let him try to teach to one child some simple fact, such as "the rose is red" in words only, and to another the same thing by bringing the rose concretely before him and then taking it away while he tries to reproduce it, say with coloured chalk and see which method goes deeper and produces more lasting effect!

At seven or eight years of age, however, even the most backward child leaves the Kinder-garten. Yet he can not at this early age be ready for the four years of parallel courses in wood, metal and clay, of which Dr. Henderson speaks in such detail. From this time till the boy or girl is ten, or twelve, there is need of some link with manual training, in order to feed the faculty that will then be required, without imposing a physical effort that there is not strength to meet. This is what is known as the transition or preparatory stage of the education. It is of course assumed that the whole course of teaching throughout the child's day is being made as largely concrete as possible, that geography, for instance, is being taught with sand and clay, for the modelling of relief-maps; that botany and national history are taught in such a way as to involve the use of pencil and paint-brush; and still there is need of something that subserves the sole end of developing the hand to quick and accurate measurement and in dealing with a gradually increasing muscular resistance and the brain to a rapid thinking out of difficulties in material. In American schools, this link is supplied by such subjects as cardboard-modelling and *Sloyd*.

In cardboard-modelling a child uses, as tools, a pencil, a measuring-ruler, pair of compasses and a good stout knife. The cardboard itself, at first, can be chequered, that is, marked with printed squares. On this, the child learns to measure from dictation a small box and the lid for the box and then to cut there, making the necessary half-depth incision for folding edges and complete cuts for separate pieces. After the ordinary four-sided box, a pentagonal box, with its lid, is made, and then one form after another, till at last even the octagonal shape is made and mastered. After this, the child can take up small articles of daily use, an envelope, a stationery-stand, a toy, a purse and what not, and make them, as an exercise of free and spontaneous activity.

From the cardboard-modelling, he passes on to *Sloyd*, a simple but severely scientific and educational form of carpentering, which can be taught, in its elementary stages, almost in an ordinary school-room and requires a carpenter's hench and a few more expensive tools, a little later. *Sloyd* was systematised and worked out as an educational subject, some ten or fifteen years ago at a place called Naas, in Sweden. And to this day teachers have to go there for training and diplomas. A few Indian teachers might be sent to learn *Sloyd* and return to popularize it here, with great advantage. In the *Sloyd* course, a number of wooden objects called "models" are produced in miniature in the schoolroom. Amongst these may be, for instance, a pointer (a tapering stick very carefully made), a paper-knife, a pencil (not, of course, inserting the writing-point), a wooden tile or mat, a frame, a block in imitation of a book, and so on. In another course might be given more complicated forms, such as, a model of a folding blotting-book, a T-square, a candlestick, a small *chouki*, a towel-rail, a window-frame, and so on. All these models, when plaining and sand-papering are complete, are expected to be correct to so fine a fraction as one-sixty-fourth of an inch, so that the educational value of the course may be easily understood.

But although Naas is the head and centre of the formulated course in Sloyd and its diplomas, there is no reason in the world why Indian schoolrooms should wait for the permission of Naas in order to create their own course in this subject. Before Sloyd became the systematised subject that it is now, it must have gone through a long experimental stage in which (1) teachers themselves were learning the secret of carpentering ; (2) trying to adopt what they had learnt to the needs of the schoolroom ; (3) reducing their conclusions to that strict geometrical and numerical analysis which makes Sloyd what it is to day. Why should Indian teachers not restore this *experimental* stage? Recognising the principles of the manual training involved, why should they not deliberately aim at creating an Indian Sloyd, as an educational course? For my own part, I believe that a few prizes and scholarships offered by some Native State,—with due tendency to prefer the State's own subjects, thrown open to the country as a whole,—would be sufficient to give birth to numerous most desirable attempts.

Public spirit in the West is, in this sense, highly developed and Governments and municipalities incorporate a new educational feature, only after it has been well tested and sounded by private persons. In America a rich woman, known as Mrs. Qunery Shaw, experimented in Sloyd training for two years at her own private cost, and then made over the results of her experiments to the State of Massachusetts, as soon as she had succeeded in proving the beneficial character of the work! Parallel efforts are made in India by occasional rich merchants, or by princes. But the activity needs indefinite extension. And we have not sufficiently recognised here that what one of us alone is not rich enough to do, five or six acting in concert, can. A group of townsmen, recognising their own children's need of deeper education, might surely make sacrifices for the sake of accomplishing such an end. They might support a promising young teacher in a modest way, while working out a neecssary course ; or they might even,—though this I do not think by any means a necessity in such cases,—go so far as to depute men to the West, for the sake of bringing back the results of Western experience.

It is clear that what is needed for this task is men who understand education in a broad sense. A certain intellectual and literary culture therefore is essential. But this by itself would be utterly useless, unless there is also some power of actual *doing*, some accuracy and dexterity of workmanship, and some slight mathematical bent.

It is in the first generation of such attempts that genius, or the fervour which amounts to genius, is most necessary. And I think, if I were an Indian prince seeking men to send West for training, I should look for them in art-schools, in architect's and engineer's offices, or even in medical colleges or scientific laboratories. Culture of mind there must be. But proved aptitude of hand is almost more a necessity still.

APPENDIX

Table showing a plan of the arrangement of the course of work in a Manual Training High School. (Ref.: Page 142, line 22).

PERIOD.	DRAWING AND ART.	WOOD-WORK.	METAL-WORK.
First year	Drawing : Freehand.	BENCH-WORK : Here a boy learns to master tools and materials and to do fine carpentering and joining.	VICE-WORK : Filling, cutting, and fitting of solid metal.
Second year	Mechanical. Architectural.	TURNING : The use of the lathes, production of round and sperical forms.	FORGING & BLACK-SMITHING : Sometimes including forms of beauty, as in wrought iron.
Third year	Clay Modelling.	PATTERN-MAKING : Wooden "forms" correct to small fractions of an inch for metal casting.	TIN-SMITHING : All sorts of cans, lamps, cases &c. are cut out and put together.
Fourth year	Wood-Carving.	Wood-Carving.	MACHINE CONSTRUCTION : In this branch we have the assembling together of all the others.